Faith

Life Together Resources

Building Character Together series

Authenticity: Living a Spiritually Healthy Life

Friendship: Living a Connected Life

Faith: Living a Transformed Life

Service: Living a Meaningful Life

Influence: Living a Contagious Life

Obedience: Living a Yielded Life

Doing Life Together series

Beginning Life Together

Connecting with God's Family

Growing to Be Like Christ

Developing Your SHAPE to Serve Others

Sharing Your Life Mission Every Day

Surrendering Your Life to God's Pleasure

Experiencing Christ Together series

Beginning in Christ Together

Connecting in Christ Together

Growing in Christ Together

Serving Like Christ Together

Sharing Christ Together

Surrendering to Christ Together

building
CHARACTER
together

FAITH

living a
Transformed
life

BRETT and DEE EASTMAN
TODD and DENISE WENDORFF

ZONDERVAN®

ZONDERVAN.com/
AUTHORTRACKER
follow your favorite authors

Faith
Copyright © 2007 by Brett and Deanna Eastman, Todd and Denise Wendorff

Requests for information should be addressed to:
Zondervan, *Grand Rapids, Michigan 49530*

ISBN-10: 0-310-24992-9
ISBN-13: 978-0-310-24992-4

Interior design by Melissa Elenbaas

Printed in the United States of America

07 08 09 10 11 12 13 • 10 9 8 7 6 5 4 3 2 1

Contents

ACKNOWLEDGMENTS

It's been quite a ride ever since our first series was published back in 2002. Literally thousands of churches and small groups have studied the LIFE TOGETHER series to the tune of over two million copies sold. As we said back in our first series, "By the grace of God and a clear call on the hearts of a few, our dream has become a reality." Now, our dream has entered the realm of being beyond all that we could ask or imagine.

To see thousands and thousands of people step out to gather a few friends and do a Bible study with an easy-to-use DVD curriculum has been amazing. People have grown in their faith, introduced their friends to Christ, and found deeper connection with God. Thanks to God for planting this idea in our hearts. Thanks to all of those who took a risk by stepping out to lead a group for six weeks for the very first time. This has been truly amazing.

Once again, a great team was instrumental to creating this new series in community. From the start back at Saddleback with Todd and Denise Wendorff and Brett and Dee Eastman, the writing team has grown. Special thanks to John Fischer, yes, THE John Fischer, for writing all of the introductions to these studies. Also, thanks to our LIFE TOGETHER writing team: Pam Marotta, Peggy Matthews Rose, and Teri Haymaker. Last, but not least, thanks to Allen White for keeping this project on track and getting the ball in the net.

Thank you to our church families who have loved and supported us and helped us grow over the years. There are so many pastors, staff, and members that have taught us so much. We love you all.

Finally, thank you to our beloved families who have lived with us, laughed at us, and loved us through it all. We love doing our lives together with you.

OUTLINE OF EACH SESSION

Most people want to live a healthy, balanced spiritual life, but few achieve this by themselves. And most small groups struggle to balance all of God's purposes in their meetings. Groups tend to overemphasize one of the five purposes, perhaps fellowship or discipleship. Rarely is there a healthy balance that includes evangelism, ministry, and worship. That's why we've included all of these elements in this study so you can live a healthy, balanced spiritual life over time.

A typical group session will include the following:

CONNECTING WITH GOD'S FAMILY (FELLOWSHIP). The foundation for spiritual growth is an intimate connection with God and his family. A few people who really know you and who earn your trust provide a place to experience the life Jesus invites you to live. This section of each session typically offers you two options: You can get to know your whole group by using the icebreaker question, or you can check in with one or two group members—your spiritual partner(s)—for a deeper connection and encouragement in your spiritual journey.

GROWING TO BE LIKE CHRIST (DISCIPLESHIP). Here is where you come face-to-face with Scripture. In core passages you'll explore what the Bible teaches about character through the lives of God's people in Scripture. The focus won't be on accumulating information but on how we should live in light of the Word of God. We want to help you apply the Scriptures practically, creatively, and from your heart as well as your head. At the end of the day, allowing the timeless truths from God's Word to transform our lives in Christ is our greatest aim.

FOR DEEPER STUDY. If you want to dig deeper into more Bible passages about the topic at hand, we've provided additional passages and questions. Your group may choose to do study homework ahead of each meeting in order to cover more biblical material. Or you as an individual may choose to study the For Deeper Study passages on your own. If you prefer not to do study homework, the Growing section will

provide you with plenty to discuss within the group. These options allow individuals or the whole group to go deeper in their study, while still accommodating those who can't do homework.

You can record your discoveries in your journal. We encourage you to read some of your insights to a friend (spiritual partner) for accountability and support. Spiritual partners may check in each week over the phone, through email, or at the beginning of the group meeting.

 DEVELOPING YOUR GIFTS TO SERVE OTHERS (MINISTRY). Jesus trained his disciples to discover and develop their gifts to serve others. God has designed you uniquely to serve him in a way no other person can. This section will help you discover and use your God-given design. It will also encourage your group to discover your unique design as a community. In this study, you'll put into practice what you've learned in the Bible study by taking a step to serve others. These simple steps will take your group on a faith journey that could change your lives forever.

 SHARING YOUR LIFE MISSION EVERY DAY (EVANGELISM). Many people skip over this aspect of the Christian life because it's scary, relationally awkward, or simply too much work for their busy schedules. But Jesus wanted all of his disciples to help outsiders connect with him, to know him personally. This doesn't mean preaching on street corners. It could mean welcoming a few newcomers into your group, hosting a short-term group in your home, or walking through this study with a friend. In this study, you'll have an opportunity to go beyond Bible study to biblical living.

 SURRENDERING YOUR LIFE FOR GOD'S PLEASURE (WORSHIP). God is most pleased by a heart that is fully his. Each group session will give you a chance to surrender your heart to God in prayer and worship. You may read a psalm together, share a page in your journal, or sing a song to close your meeting. (A LIFE TOGETHER Worship DVD/CD series, produced by Maranatha!, is available through www.lifetogether. com.) If you have never prayed aloud in a group before, no one will put pressure on you. Instead, you'll experience the support of others who are praying for you. This time will knit your hearts in community and help you surrender your hurts and dreams into the hands of the One who knows you best.

STUDY NOTES. This section provides background notes on the Bible passage(s) you examine in the Growing section. You may want to refer to these notes during your group meeting or as a reference for those doing additional study.

REFLECTIONS. Each week on the Reflections pages we provide Scriptures to read and reflect on between group meetings. We suggest you use this section to seek God at home throughout the week. This time at home should begin and end with prayer. Don't get in a hurry; take enough time to hear God's direction.

SUBGROUPS FOR DISCUSSION AND PRAYER. In some of the sessions of this series we have suggested you separate into groups of two to four for discussion or prayer. This is to assure greater participation and deeper discussion.

FAITH THAT WORKS — ABRAHAM AND ISAAC

Having faith means putting yourself in a place where God can work, and one of those places is in fellowship with other believers. "For where two or three have gathered together in My name, I am there in their midst" (Matthew 18:20 NASB). That's why we do this. We are believing and expecting God to be in the middle of our small group, and we are gathering in faith to experience that reality. Getting here is an act of faith. Expecting something from God is an act of faith. This is not a self-help group or a group that believes strength is in numbers. The sum of the parts is not greater than the whole. It's this: When the parts get together, something miraculous happens: God shows up.

God showed up on the mountain, waiting for Abraham to arrive to sacrifice his son Isaac. Imagine what would have happened if God hadn't shown up, hadn't provided the ram instead. It would have been all over. No children of Israel. No Savior of the world. No hope for mankind. Abraham packed all his stuff together, gathered Isaac, and took off for the mountain expecting to meet God there — and he was not disappointed. We will come to these meetings the same way. We will expect to meet God here and we will not be disappointed.

I've heard of a group of guys that gets together regularly at a Starbucks somewhere in New Jersey, only they have changed the name of the place to St. Arbucks. That's perfect. That means that for once a week, Starbucks is turned into a cathedral inclusive of the presence of God. That's because these guys gather by faith, and for a few hours a week, the local Starbucks becomes St. Arbucks of New Jersey. Maybe you should think about renaming your place of meeting!

CONNECTING WITH GOD'S FAMILY   20 MIN.

As much as we may wish we could avoid life's difficult times, it is only through the purification process that full-bodied faith is produced. Saying we believe is one thing ... but how will we respond when what we say must become what we do? Will we be full-tread Christians, or is our faith merely in our mouths? Paul tells us in

Romans 4:1–5 that faith justifies us before God. He further declares that our salvation does not come through works, but by believing in the One who justifies the ungodly—the condition we are all in before Christ is invited into our lives. Where, then, do works come in? In this session, we'll look at James' challenge to consider lessons from the lives of two Old Testament figures who demonstrated growing, living faith—faith in action.

1. From time to time, we all face situations that seem impossible. Share what happened during an "impossible" moment in your life. How did God use others in your life to bring you through, and what did he teach you from it all?

2. Scene: You are on your way to your car in the parking lot when you pass a friend whose car won't start. What do you say to your friend?

3. Open to the Small Group Agreement on pages 89–90. Take a few minutes to review the values listed there and make some decisions regarding your expectations for this study. A little bit of time spent on this today could save a lot of confusion and disappointment over unmet expectations throughout the next several weeks. Also, glance through the Frequently Asked Questions on pages 86–88 to discover some of the solutions and strategies we suggest for common problems groups face.

4. We recommend that you rotate host homes on a regular basis and let the hosts lead the group discussion. We've come to realize that healthy groups rotate leadership. This helps to develop every member's ability to shepherd a few people in a safe environment. Even Jesus gave others the opportunity to serve alongside him (Mark 6:30–44). In session three we will explain how to set up a rotating schedule.

Collect phone numbers and email addresses from your small group members so that you can touch base, if needed, between group meetings. The Small Group Roster on pages 118–119 is a good place to keep this information. While you are working through this session, pass your study guides around the circle and have group members fill in their contact information.

GROWING IN YOUR SPIRITUAL JOURNEY   40 MIN.

James wanted his readers to understand the vital underpinning of faith: it must be active to be alive. Anyone can say they believe. But can they prove it? That, he said, is the real test of faith.

Since he addressed primarily Jewish Christians, he pointed to examples from the Scriptures. God asked Abraham to sacrifice the son he had waited so many years to hold in his arms—the son of God's promise (Genesis 17:19), through whom he would become father of many nations (15:5; 17:6–8). Abraham proved he believed God by his willingness to do what God asked, even when it made no sense.

How will the world know we believe unless we prove it through what we do? We will not always, or often, understand God's tests. What matters is our willingness to obey.

Read James 2:17b–26:

Faith by itself, if it is not accompanied by action, is dead.
[18]But someone will say, "You have faith; I have deeds."
Show me your faith without deeds, and I will show you
my faith by what I do. [19]You believe that there is one God.
Good! Even the demons believe that—and shudder. [20]You
foolish man, do you want evidence that faith without deeds
is useless? [21]Was not our ancestor Abraham considered
righteous for what he did when he offered his son Isaac on
the altar? [22]You see that his faith and his actions were work-
ing together, and his faith was made complete by what he
did. [23]And the scripture was fulfilled that says, "Abraham
believed God, and it was credited to him as righteousness,"
and he was called God's friend. [24]You see that a person is
justified by what he does and not by faith alone. [25]In the
same way, was not even Rahab the prostitute considered

*righteous for what she did when she gave lodging to the spies
and sent them off in a different direction? *26*As the body
without the spirit is dead, so faith without deeds is dead.*

5. What does verse 22 say about the result of Abraham's
   actions? How did those actions demonstrate Abraham's faith?

6. What does verse 23 say about Abraham? What was credited
   to him as righteousness?

7. What does it usually take for us to learn to trust God?

8. Verse 23b says of Abraham, "he was called God's friend."
   Does God call you friend? How can you know?

9. In verse 20, James is adamant about the relationship between
   faith and deeds, or actions. What does he say about faith and
   action in verse 17b?

10. Some people think James 2:18 contradicts Paul's teaching
    in Romans 3:28: "For we maintain that a man is justified by
    faith apart from observing the law." But read on! Who else
    believes in God (James 2:19)? How do you think acting on
    our faith gives it life?

11. Has your faith ever been tested as was Abraham's? Go around the group and briefly share an example or two. What did you learn from your experience?

FOR DEEPER STUDY

Read about the strenuous test of Abraham's faith in Genesis 22:1 – 19.

What do you think is meant in verse 8? How would God provide the lamb?

Why would God ask Abraham to sacrifice this son of his promise? Was he just being cruel?

How was Abraham's faith impacted by this event?

DEVELOPING YOUR GIFTS FOR LIFE   10 MIN.

12. In spite of the fact that Abraham wavered a time or two along the way, it's clear he had the spiritual gift of faith. Whether or not faith is your primary gift, Scripture tells us that each of us has been given a measure of faith (Romans 12:3). How have you seen God grow your faith through service to others? Share a story with your group as an encouragement.

13. Most people want to live a healthy, balanced life. A regular medical checkup is a good way to measure health and spot potential problems. In the same way, a spiritual checkup is vital to your spiritual well-being. The Personal Health Assessment was designed to give you a quick snapshot, or pulse, of your spiritual health. Take a few minutes alone to complete the assessment found on pages 96–97 of the appendix. After answering each question, tally your results. We will use the Personal Health Assessment throughout this study to plan and track your progress.

14. Having an accountability partner is a great way to keep us on track and provides opportunity to grow together spiritually. Pair up with someone in your group (we suggest that men partner with men and women with women) to be your "spiritual partner" during this study. He or she doesn't have to be your best friend but will simply encourage you to complete the goals you set for yourself throughout this study. Following through on a resolution is tough when you're on your own, but we've found it makes all the difference to have a partner cheering us on.

On pages 92–93 is a Personal Health Plan, a chart for keeping track of your spiritual progress. In the box that says "WHO are you connecting with spiritually?" write your partner's name. When you check in with your partner each week, the "Partner's Progress" column on this chart will provide a place to record your partner's progress in the step he or she chose.

If you have more than one partner, ask your leader for an extra Personal Health Plan. For now, don't worry about the WHAT, WHERE, WHEN, and HOW questions on the Health Plan.

SHARING YOUR LIFE MISSION EVERYDAY   10 MIN.

Because of Abraham's faith, a nation was born. Where does God want to use your story of faith?

15. Who do you know who needs to come to faith in Christ? Use the Circles of Life diagram on the next page to help identify neighbors, family members, friends, or coworkers who you

can begin to pray for. Write at least two names in each circle. Be sure to pray for them during the the Surrendering section prayer time.

CIRCLES OF LIFE

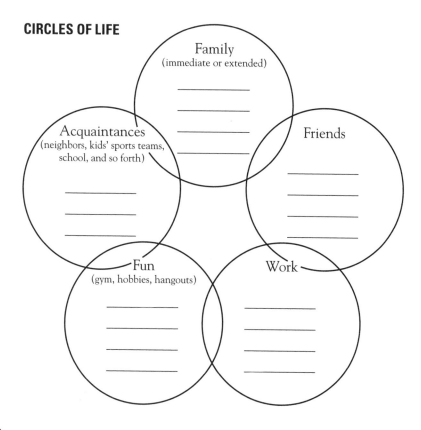

![Praying hands icon] **SURRENDERING** YOUR LIFE FOR GOD'S PLEASURE   15–20 MIN.

"Now faith," says Hebrews 11:1, "is being sure of what we hope for and certain of what we do not see."

16. Is there someone you have hoped would come to a saving knowledge of Christ, or is there a circumstance you've been longing to see resolved? God is pleased by the demonstration of our faith through prayer. Write the name or circumstance below and share your prayer request with the group.

17. Finish this session by praying for each other. Don't forget to pray for the names in your Circles of Life from question 15. Record prayer requests on the Prayer and Praise Report on page 21 and pray for them throughout the week.

18. Note the Reflections pages at the end of this session. These have been provided to use daily during the course of this study. Each day there is a reading of Scripture from the study. Record your thoughts in the space provided below each Scripture.

STUDY NOTES

Faith. Moral conviction. In the New Testament, faith is believing, trusting in something or someone reliable. Behind faith is a strong conviction of the one who can be trusted.

Faith and his actions were working together. Faith and actions are both efficacious (effective) and inseparable. Paul tends to emphasize the worthlessness of pre-conversion works (Ephesians 2:8–9) while James emphasizes the worth of post-conversion works. Works never constitute saving faith but they do validate saving faith. See Ephesians 2:10.

Credited to him. To take into account, to take an inventory. God took into account Abraham's faith and found it worthy of righteousness. His faith was weighty because he acted on it.

Righteousness. Both in 2 Chronicles 20:7 and Isaiah 41:8, Abraham is called a friend of God. He was right before God or made righteous. Christ's righteousness (perfection) is placed on us as a robe. We inherit his righteousness by faith.

Justified. It's a legal declaration of guiltlessness by a merciful and gracious judge; a pronouncement of righteousness. Jesus' atoning work on the cross appeased the anger of God and ransomed us from sin and guilt. We went from being enemies of God to becoming friends of God.

Briefly share your prayer requests with the large group, making notations below. Then gather in small groups of two to four to pray for each other.

Date: _____

PRAYER REQUESTS

_____

_____

_____

_____

_____

_____

_____

_____

_____

_____

_____

PRAISE REPORT

_____

_____

_____

_____

_____

_____

_____

_____

REFLECTIONS

Each day read the daily verse(s) and give prayerful consideration to what you learn about God, his Spirit, and his place in your life. Then record your thoughts, insights, or prayer in the Reflect section. On day six record a summary of what you have learned over the entire week through this study.

DAY 1   *"The apostles said to the Lord, 'Increase our faith!' He replied, 'If you have faith as small as a mustard seed, you can say to this mulberry tree, "Be uprooted and planted in the sea," and it will obey you.'" (Luke 17:5–6)*

REFLECT: _____

_____

_____

_____

_____

_____

_____

_____

DAY 2   *"And the scripture was fulfilled that says, 'Abraham believed God, and it was credited to him as righteousness,' and he was called God's friend." (James 2:23)*

REFLECT: _____

_____

_____

_____

_____

_____

_____

_____

DAY 3   *"Now when a man works, his wages are not credited to him as a gift, but as an obligation. However, to the man who does not work but trusts God who justifies the wicked, his faith is credited as righteousness." (Romans 4:4–5)*

REFLECT: _____

_____

_____

_____

_____

_____

_____

_____

_____

_____

_____

DAY 4   *"For by the grace given me I say to every one of you: Do not think of yourself more highly than you ought, but rather think of yourself with sober judgment, in accordance with the measure of faith God has given you." (Romans 12:3)*

REFLECT: _____

_____

_____

_____

_____

_____

_____

_____

_____

_____

DAY 5   *"Now faith is being sure of what we hope for and certain of what we do not see." (Hebrews 11:1)*

REFLECT: _____

_____

_____

_____

_____

_____

_____

_____

_____

_____

_____

DAY 6   Use the following space to write any thoughts God has put in your heart and mind about the things discussed during session one and/or during your Reflections time this week.

SUMMARY: _____

_____

_____

_____

_____

_____

_____

_____

_____

_____

_____

FAITH THAT LISTENS — MARY AND MARTHA

"Be still and know that I am God" (Psalm 46:10). There are many ways to do this, but one of the most meaningful to me has been close proximity to God's creation, whether it be the ocean, the mountains, the desert, the local park or arboretum — virtually anyplace you can get to where you can be surrounded by what God has made, as opposed to man-made things.

In my younger days I could take time for this on a somewhat regular basis. Then we get older and responsibilities set in and family obligations take over, and suddenly, I realized it's been years since I sat and heard the ocean, or walked through a forest, or smelled the wind in the pines. To be sure, it's not just doing these things; it is being God-conscious when you do them. To watch the sunset and imagine him as the painter. To listen to a brook and imagine his truth bubbling over the rocks of hard days and nights. To taste the ocean spray and feel his ever-present power in the incessant pounding of the waves.

What is life for, if not for this? When you finally get to the feet of Jesus, it's amazing how your perspective changes. Of course, you can get to the feet of Jesus anytime, anywhere. It doesn't take a forest to get there. But I have found that being around what God has made helps simplify the process. Think of it as a firsthand experience with the Creator. It's a primary experience unmediated by man. So sit and listen and speak, but don't speak too soon. Listen first.

How could we ever be too busy for that for which we were made?

CONNECTING WITH GOD'S FAMILY   20 MIN.

Faith reveals itself in our actions, but it is often built in the quiet moments we spend sitting at the feet of Jesus. We live in an era of busyness, often rushing through life and getting nowhere! In this session we'll deliberately take time to understand the relationship between faith and focus.

1. Talk about a time when you needed someone's attention and they were too busy or preoccupied to give you what you

needed. Or (if you're brave enough), share a time when a project distracted you from paying attention to someone, like a spouse or a child, who needed your time. Which is likely to be remembered longer: the project or the pain? Why?

2. What would you do if the president of the United States called and said he was coming to dinner at your house this week? (Let your conversation respect the office, even if you might or might not respect the office holder.)

3. Check in with your spiritual partner(s), or with another partner if yours is absent. Turn to the Personal Health Assessment on pages 96–97 and review the Growing section. Choose one area in which you need to grow and set a goal for making progress in that area. Then turn to the Personal Health Plan on pages 92–93. In the box that says "WHAT is your next step for growth?" write one step you need to take to accomplish the goal you set for yourself.

Tell your partner what step you chose. When you check in with your partner each week, the "Partner's Progress" column on this chart will provide a place to record your partner's progress in the step he or she chose.

GROWING IN YOUR SPIRITUAL JOURNEY 40 MIN.

Martha and Mary typify the often opposite contrasts in our individual natures. Through Jesus' patient attitude toward the busy Martha, he causes her, and his future readers, to pause and consider what really matters.

Martha clearly had the gift of hospitality, but with it she displays clear warning signs of a first-century workaholic! She is the classic overachiever, the doer whose personality goes out of control when she perceives that others aren't "doing their part"—whatever she thinks that part should be. Mary, on the other hand, recognized and fully embraced the unique opportunity she had to spend time with and learn from Jesus.

Through Mary, Jesus shows us the need to take time out from our daily schedule to focus on our Lord, to learn from him and discover what really matters.

Read Luke 10:38–42:

> As Jesus and his disciples were on their way, he came to a village where a woman named Martha opened her home to him. [39]She had a sister called Mary, who sat at the Lord's feet listening to what he said. [40]But Martha was distracted by all the preparations that had to be made. She came to him and asked, "Lord, don't you care that my sister has left me to do the work by myself? Tell her to help me!" [41]"Martha, Martha," the Lord answered, "you are worried and upset about many things, [42]but only one thing is needed. Mary has chosen what is better, and it will not be taken away from her."

4. Is it wrong to be busy in our work for the Lord? What is the difference between being busy *for* the Lord and being busy *with* the Lord?

5. In verse 40, Martha said to Jesus, "Lord, don't you care … ?" Have you ever found yourself wondering that same thing? Share a story of a time you were worn out with serving and wondered if God really cared.

6. Do any of you have an example of the fruit of waiting on Christ? What great truths have you learned as you waited on his timing?

7. How does the story of Martha and Mary show us the heart of Christ? What kind of master is he? Read the truth about what matters to God in 1 Samuel 16:7.

8. Reflect on Jesus' words to Martha in verses 41–42a. What are you worried about? How could a decision to let go of your worry and spend time with Christ each day impact your situation? Why not make that decision now? To reinforce your decision, look at examples from the life of Jesus in Matthew 14:13, 23; Mark 1:35; and Luke 5:16. Jesus frequently slipped away to spend time with the Father.

FOR DEEPER STUDY

Look at John 11:17–44, where we once again encounter Mary and Martha. What did Martha say to Jesus in verse 21? How is this similar to her complaint in Luke 10:40? How do her words in John 11:27 reflect her spiritual growth?

DEVELOPING YOUR GIFTS TO SERVE OTHERS   10 MIN.

9. Would you describe yourself as a Martha or as a Mary? No matter our gender, we each tend to be stronger in one of the two traits. Our gifts for serving need to be balanced with the peace of knowing Christ and letting his life shine though us as we serve others. Ask God to help you, and record what you receive from the Lord either in the space provided or, better yet, in a journal. (If you're interested in journaling, be sure to read the Journaling 101 section on page 98 to gain

insight into how to integrate God's Word and journaling into your devotional time, allowing you to focus your time to receive specific direction from the Lord.)

10. Plan a time for your group to throw a party for Jesus. Imagine he has come to your town and said to your group, "I'd love to stop by and visit with you! I'm coming to your small group next week." Use this occasion as an opportunity to learn your individual tendencies and be open to discussion for finding balance in your lives. Discuss whether your group would like to have a potluck or other type of social event to celebrate Jesus' presence in your group. It could be as simple as planning a meal prior to a group meeting or planning to celebrate the completion of this study with a special "social" meeting.

 SHARING YOUR LIFE MISSION EVERY DAY   10 MIN.

11. Whether our work is in the home or outside our home, each of us regularly comes into contact with people who need to see Christ in us. When people watch you, who are they most likely to see? Do they witness a Martha, always busy rushing to meet deadlines? Or do they see a Mary, someone who has spent time preparing for the day by connecting with Christ? If you're not sure whether or not people see Jesus in you, ask the Lord to reveal himself through your life. Then be ready to hear and obey his instructions.

12. Turn to the Personal Health Assessment on pages 96–97. Take turns sharing one area where you would like to grow in sharing God's love in your everyday life. Identify one step you can take to make progress in the area you chose. Record this step under the "WHEN are you shepherding another in Christ?" question on your Personal Health Plan on page 92.

SURRENDERING YOUR LIFE FOR GOD'S PLEASURE   15–20 MIN.

13. Has this lesson convicted you of the need to stop being so busy *doing* for God and start spending more time *being with* Jesus? Confess that to him right now as your group prays together. You don't have to say it out loud, but a verbal confession can have cleansing power. As we saw in our first study in this series, our actions should be the physical, outward expression of our faith, but they must be inspired *by* that faith. When our hearts and lives are surrendered to God, he fills us with the ability to see what he wants us to do and gives us the will to obey. The surrendered life is a life empowered *by* God to live *for* God.

14. Read John 11:5 and note what it says about Jesus' feelings toward Martha, Mary, and Lazarus. Is there someone in your life who frustrates you by being either, (1) too busy, too fussy, too perfectionistic; or (2) too laid back, unaware of their own inability to engage with the things of life? How can you surrender that person to God today, and love them anyway? Maybe that person is more like Lazarus—dead to the world for all practical purposes. Where can you trust Jesus to raise him or her to new life?

15. Take a few minutes to discuss how you can make the most of praying for one another. Is there someone in your group who would like to coordinate prayer for this study? This would mean making sure prayer doesn't get forgotten, recording requests and praises, starting a prayer chain, or emailing prayer requests between meetings. Make prayer a priority and be sure to celebrate God's answers to prayer at the end of the study. Make a habit of recording your prayer requests in the Prayer and Praise Report found at the end of each session in this guide.

16. Use the Reflections verses at the end of this session in your quiet time this week. Record any thoughts or direction you receive from the Lord in the space provided.

STUDY NOTES

Martha and Mary. These two sisters had a brother named Lazarus whom Jesus raised from the dead in John 11. They were close friends of Jesus. Jesus had close friends, besides his disciples whom he loved. It shows the human connection side of our Lord and Savior.

Sat at Jesus' feet. It would have been customary for young rabbinic students to sit at the feet of a rabbi to hear his teaching, but never a woman. A woman's place was to serve and be separate. Jesus broke this barrier and made himself available to all people. It was a posture of respect and deep spiritual interest.

Distracted, worried, and upset. All words describing the emotional turmoil inside Martha. Worry is *wurgen* in German. It means "to strangle or to choke."

Chosen what is better. Often seen as a rebuke but more importantly, a clarification of importance. It was the better of two options at this time. Finding time for Jesus is always a matter of priority and importance, even in the midst of responsibilities.

Listening. Listening requires understanding. One hears by intently listening for meaning in what is being said. How well do we listen when others talk? The use of this word implies the posture and attitude of Mary. She was intent on hearing what Jesus had to say. Worry is the opposite of listening (see Psalm 46:10).

PRAYER AND PRAISE REPORT

Briefly share your prayer requests with the large group, making notations below.
Then gather in small groups of two to four to pray for each other.

Date: _____

PRAYER REQUESTS

_____

_____

_____

_____

_____

_____

_____

_____

_____

_____

_____

PRAISE REPORT

_____

_____

_____

_____

_____

_____

_____

_____

REFLECTIONS

Each day read the daily verse(s) and give prayerful consideration to what you learn about God, his Spirit, and his place in your life. Then record your thoughts, insights, or prayer in the Reflect section. On day six record a summary of what you have learned over the entire week through this study.

DAY 1 *"Are not two sparrows sold for a penny? Yet not one of them will fall to the ground apart from the will of your Father. And even the very hairs of your head are all numbered. So don't be afraid; you are worth more than many sparrows." (Matthew 10:29 – 31)*

REFLECT: _____

_____

_____

_____

_____

_____

_____

_____

_____

DAY 2 *"Take my yoke upon you and learn from me, for I am gentle and humble in heart, and you will find rest for your souls. For my yoke is easy and my burden is light." (Matthew 11:29 – 30)*

REFLECT: _____

_____

_____

_____

_____

_____

_____

DAY 3   *"Very early in the morning, while it was still dark, Jesus got up, left the house and went off to a solitary place, where he prayed." (Mark 1:35)*

REFLECT: _____

_____

_____

_____

_____

_____

_____

_____

_____

_____

_____

DAY 4   *"The LORD does not look at the things man looks at. Man looks at the outward appearance, but the LORD looks at the heart." (1 Samuel 16:7)*

REFLECT: _____

_____

_____

_____

_____

_____

_____

_____

_____

_____

_____

DAY 5   *"My heart is not proud, O LORD, my eyes are not haughty; I do not concern myself with great matters or things too wonderful for me. But I have stilled and quieted my soul; like a weaned child with its mother, like a weaned child is my soul within me. O Israel, put your hope in the LORD both now and forevermore." (Psalm 131:1–3)*

REFLECT: _____

_____

_____

_____

_____

_____

_____

_____

_____

_____

DAY 6   Use the following space to write any thoughts God has put in your heart and mind about the things discussed during session two and/or during your Reflections time this week.

SUMMARY: _____

_____

_____

_____

_____

_____

_____

_____

_____

_____

_____

FAITH THAT IS MULTIPLIED —
PAUL AND TIMOTHY

The best mentoring takes place "as you go." Mentoring classes can be helpful, but they are not true mentoring. When I was a young man studying for the ministry, I was an intern at a church for three years. We had classes where the various pastors taught us in the areas of their expertise, but we were also assigned, each of us, to one pastor for discipleship. As I think back, it's not the classroom I remember as much as the trips we took, the meals we ate together, and the long drives to places with my pastor that were, in many ways, more fruitful than the actual ministry we came to do.

I'll never forget one time I was with a team of pastors and laymen spending a few days speaking and sharing on a Christian college campus. In a packed dorm lounge as we were all sharing our stories, I made a comment about my pristine evangelical upbringing by saying "I used to be 'golden boy.'" To which a rather brash and vocal member of our team shouted out from the back of the room, "What do you mean, used to be?" Dumbfounded and humiliated, I staggered forward to complete my little talk, and then spent a good deal of time later with our team unpacking why he had pointed this out to me. It was incredibly personal and ultimately affirming, although painful at first, and helped me see some things about myself I may never had encountered otherwise. It's these kinds of "as you go" experiences that teach us the most about ourselves and others.

CONNECTING WITH GOD'S FAMILY   20 MIN.

Faith is like a muscle — it needs to be exercised to become and stay strong. Once his own faith was headed in the right direction, Paul recognized his responsibility to train up the younger generation. Growing faith needs to be demonstrated (session one), cultivated (session two), and passed on. When we train someone else in what we believe, we are passing it on to another, who can transfer it to another, and so on. That's the principle of multiplication. In this study, we'll consider the importance of personal training and the call on our lives to pass on what we've learned.

1. Think of a teacher who made a difference in your life. What was special about him or her? How did their investment in your life have lasting significance?

2. What difference can age make in our perspective on life?

3. Sit with your spiritual partner(s), or with another partner if yours is absent. Share how your time in God's Word went this week. How did your effort at journaling go? Have you made any progress on the goals you set in the Grow and Share purposes on the Health Plan? Be sure to record your progress and your partner's progress on page 93.

GROWING IN YOUR SPIRITUAL JOURNEY   40 MIN.

Timothy was one of the first "second generation" believers. Most scholars concur that Paul's letters to him were written just prior to Paul's final Roman imprisonment. Clearly, Paul understood that mentoring was critical to the survival of the Christian faith. Notice the emphasis on spiritual discipline in the first two passages that we're about to read.

Timothy had been brought up in a household of faith, thanks to the influence of his mother, Eunice, and his grandmother, Lois (2 Timothy 1:5). But the Scriptures say nothing of a father figure in his life until Paul enters the scene. It's clear that Paul loved Timothy as his own son (see 1 Timothy 1:2) and because of that, he undoubtedly felt responsible as an authority figure in Timothy's life. So he expended great time and energy in these letters to make sure Timothy understood what was required to live an effective, transferable Christian life and to lead an exemplary life before others.

Statistics say a generation can be lost in a matter of five years if good people do nothing. Through the story of Paul and Timothy, we learn about the critical need to mentor others in the faith.

Read 1 Timothy 4:6–16 and 1 Timothy 6:11–12:

4:6If you point these things out to the brothers, you will be a good minister of Christ Jesus, brought up in the truths of the faith and of the good teaching that you have followed. 7Have nothing to do with godless myths and old wives' tales; rather, train yourself to be godly. 8For physical training is of some value, but godliness has value for all things, holding promise for both the present life and the life to come. 9This is a trustworthy saying that deserves full acceptance 10(and for this we labor and strive), that we have put our hope in the living God, who is the Savior of all men, and especially of those who believe. 11Command and teach these things. 12Don't let anyone look down on you because you are young, but set an example for the believers in speech, in life, in love, in faith and in purity. 13Until I come, devote yourself to the public reading of Scripture, to preaching and to teaching. 14Do not neglect your gift, which was given you through a prophetic message when the body of elders laid their hands on you. 15Be diligent in these matters; give yourself wholly to them, so that everyone may see your progress. 16Watch your life and doctrine closely. Persevere in them, because if you do, you will save both yourself and your hearers.

6:11But you, man of God, flee from all this, and pursue righteousness, godliness, faith, love, endurance and gentleness. 12Fight the good fight of the faith. Take hold of the eternal life to which you were called when you made your good confession in the presence of many witnesses.

4. In 1 Timothy 4:6 Paul advises his apprentice to "point these things out to the brothers." What are "these things"? (See 1 Timothy 4:1 – 5.)

5. Similarly, from what does Paul warn Timothy to flee (see 1 Timothy 6:11)? What does he tell Timothy to pursue instead?

6. Take time in your group to identify the action words in these two passages. What do they tell you about Paul's attitude in writing this letter?

7. Look at 1 Timothy 1:18 and 4:14. In addition to Paul's fatherly connection to Timothy, what other reason did he have for training up this younger man?

8. Why is it important to pay careful attention to what we believe? What kinds of things can influence our beliefs?

9. In twenty-first-century America, postmoderns are being told anything and everything is okay. In light of that fact, why should it matter whether or not we pass on our faith in Christ?

FOR DEEPER STUDY

Paul exhorts Timothy to pursue a life of godliness. Look at the following verses and note anything you learn about pursuing godliness. Look for reasons why we should pursue godliness, how to pursue it, the results of pursuing it, and any warnings.

Proverbs 15:9

Proverbs 21:21

Isaiah 51:1

Romans 9:30–31

2 Timothy 2:22

Prayerfully consider how you would like to respond to what you have discovered. Make a plan and record it on your Health Plan on page 92 in the appendix.

DEVELOPING YOUR GIFTS TO SERVE OTHERS   10 MIN.

In our fitness-focused society, it's important to note Paul's wise comment that while "physical training is of some value ... godliness has value for all things" (1 Timothy 4:8). Physical discipline keeps us healthy for doing God's work while we are here on earth, but spiritual discipline has eternal worth.

10. What are your daily spiritual discipline practices? Share them with the group—not to show off, but to inspire. What can we do to make sure we are not ignoring the spiritual gifts within each of us?

11. "Rotating Leaders" is one of the values we highly recommend for your group. People need opportunities to experiment with ways in which God may have gifted them. Your group will

give you all the encouragement you need before, during, and after the session.

We also suggest you rotate host homes, with the host of each meeting providing the refreshments. Some groups like to let the host lead the meeting each week, while others like to let one person host while another person leads.

The Small Group Calendar on page 91 is a tool for planning who will host and lead each meeting. Take a few minutes to plan hosts and leaders for your next three meetings. Don't pass this up! It will revolutionize your group.

SHARING YOUR LIFE MISSION EVERY DAY 10 MIN.

Mentoring others involves both ministry and mission-oriented activities. We can all be like Paul, and the Scriptures encourage us to take on this role.

12. How can you leave a legacy of mentoring through your life? Consider various ways, such as:

- Working with youth

- Teaching Sunday school

- Leading others in your workplace

- Writing your story, or writing a book about what you know

    Consider volunteering in a community youth program or another area where your group can reach out to your community together.

13. Two weeks ago we used the Circles of Life to identify those around us who need to grow in their faith. Have you seen any answers to your prayers? Share these with the group. Maybe this week you will be able to share with someone in your circle the changes God is making in your life.

14. Who has God put in your life to mentor? If you have kids, consider how you can help them develop a sense of God's presence in their lives. If your kids are grown or you don't have children, is there a young person in your family, workplace, or neighborhood who might be longing to connect with you? It's easy to miss the signals—young people often give off the attitude that adults are so boring! But the truth is, we all need to learn from those who've been down the road before us.

15. What do you need to let go of in order to make time for training up a young life, or where do you need to invest in your own spiritual development? If you know of a retreat or conference coming up soon, why not sign up for yourself and invite someone else who'd be blessed by time set aside to learn about God?

16. Close your time together by praying for the needs expressed today by group members, remembering God's power is available to meet your needs. Write down group members' prayer requests on the Prayer and Praise Report provided on page 45. As God answers these requests, be sure to celebrate how he is working among and through your group.

17. Use the Reflections verses at the end of this session in your quiet time this week. Record any thoughts or direction you receive from the Lord in the space provided.

STUDY NOTES

Minister. The original Greek word *diakoneo* refers to the office or role of a deacon in the church. Their responsibilities included assisting the apostles as well as serving the poor and helping with the church's administrative needs. See Acts 6:1–6.

Training. From the Greek *gumnazo*, "to train" (mind or body), we arrive at the English word "gymnasium." Men would often meet in Jewish gymnasiums and strip down to train for athletic events. Hebrews 12:1 gives us insight into stripping encumbrances and sins to run the race. The training aspect is also seen in 1 Corinthians 9:24–27 as illustrated by the exercise or discipline needed to compete in a race or a boxing match.

Godly ... godliness. It means holiness or moral perfection. Not that we have become perfectly holy, but we strive for godliness in all our behavior (1 Peter 1:15). First Timothy 1:5 describes the goal of Christian godliness as "love ... from a pure heart and a good conscience and a sincere faith."

Diligent. To care about, tend to, and practice. This word is closely related to training. It can also mean to meditate, which implies focused thinking or continued practice with great effort. Godliness comes no other way than through practice and focused attention.

Young. Youth were not looked upon to be role models or examples in first-century society. The Greek word for "youth" (King James Version), *neotes*, could refer to any male of military age, up to age forty. Timothy was probably about thirty years old at this time. Yet, he was to present himself as a model, the Greek word *typos*, an image for others to follow.

Flee. To shun or vanish from; to seek safety by flight; to escape. Sin is not something to toy with. Instead, we are to run from it as we would run from a trap (see 1 Timothy 6:9). The sins Paul describes produce the exact opposite of what he is hoping to build in Timothy.

Fight the good fight of the faith. This is a military expression that describes the perseverance of the believer. The Christian life is often described as a fight or a war. We war against principalities and powers (2 Corinthians 10:4–5). There will be one final war in heaven that the Lamb will fight for us to overcome the forces of darkness (Revelation 17:14).

Briefly share your prayer requests with the large group, making notations below. Then gather in small groups of two to four to pray for each other.

Date: _____

PRAYER REQUESTS

_____

_____

_____

_____

_____

_____

_____

_____

_____

_____

_____

_____

PRAISE REPORT

_____

_____

_____

_____

_____

_____

_____

_____

REFLECTIONS

Each day read the daily verse(s) and give prayerful consideration to what you learn about God, his Spirit, and his place in your life. Then record your thoughts, insights, or prayer in the Reflect section. On day six record a summary of what you have learned over the entire week through this study.

DAY 1   *"This is a trustworthy saying that deserves full acceptance (and for this we labor and strive), that we have put our hope in the living God, who is the Savior of all men, and especially of those who believe." (1 Timothy 4:9 – 10)*

REFLECT: _____

_____

_____

_____

_____

_____

_____

DAY 2   *"Command and teach these things. Don't let anyone look down on you because you are young, but set an example for the believers in speech, in life, in love, in faith and in purity. Until I come, devote yourself to the public reading of Scripture, to preaching and to teaching. Do not neglect your gift, which was given you through a prophetic message when the body of elders laid their hands on you." (1 Timothy 4:11 – 14)*

REFLECT: _____

_____

_____

_____

_____

_____

_____

DAY 3 *"Be diligent in these matters; give yourself wholly to them, so that everyone may see your progress. Watch your life and doctrine closely. Persevere in them, because if you do, you will save both yourself and your hearers." (1 Timothy 4:15 – 16)*

REFLECT: _____

_____

_____

_____

_____

_____

_____

_____

_____

_____

DAY 4 *"In the presence of God and of Christ Jesus, who will judge the living and the dead, and in view of his appearing and his kingdom, I give you this charge: Preach the Word; be prepared in season and out of season; correct, rebuke and encourage — with great patience and careful instruction." (2 Timothy 4:1 – 2)*

REFLECT: _____

_____

_____

_____

_____

_____

_____

_____

_____

_____

DAY 5   *"Pray also for me, that whenever I open my mouth, words may be given me so that I will fearlessly make known the mystery of the gospel, for which I am an ambassador in chains. Pray that I may declare it fearlessly, as I should." (Ephesians 6:19–20)*

REFLECT: _____

_____

_____

_____

_____

_____

_____

_____

_____

_____

DAY 6   Use the following space to write any thoughts God has put in your heart and mind about the things discussed during session three and/ or during your Reflections time this week.

SUMMARY: _____

_____

_____

_____

_____

_____

_____

_____

_____

_____

_____

_____

FAITH THAT OBEYS — JOSHUA

When my wife, Marti, and I were first dating, she let me know early on that she had been married and divorced — a brief one-year affair that was doomed from the start. I was not that concerned, especially since all this had taken place before she was a Christian. That bit of information seemed to satisfy all my trusted friends and counselors, save one — the wife of our senior pastor, who was concerned that a lot of easy divorces were diminishing the seriousness of marriage. God's Word says that two become one irrespective of faith or lack thereof. When it was determined that Marti had not heard from her former husband for four years before I came into the picture, the pastor's wife asked me a question I couldn't answer. If two become one and yet are torn apart, what would God's first order of business be but to restore that oneness? And what if Marti's former husband had become a Christian in the meantime, as she had? What would I do if I found out he had experienced a change of heart and desired reconciliation? Didn't I have a responsibility to at least find that out before moving on with this relationship?

I believed that God was speaking to me through this counsel, so I told Marti she needed to contact her former husband to find out his story before we could feel there was a green light for our relationship. This precipitated one of the hardest tests of obedience I have experienced with anyone. Marti has a way of expecting the worst. So for her to obey this request meant, in her mind, not that she might have to go back to her former marriage, but that she would, in fact, be going back — no question. And though this turned out not to be the case (we found out he was happily remarried), for her to be willing to do this was an act of sheer trust and obedience.

Obedience that produces character is based on trust that God has our best interests at heart even when it doesn't look like it to us.

CONNECTING WITH GOD'S FAMILY   20 MIN.

It's one thing to know God has promised us an answer to our prayers — and quite another to take hold of that answer. All too often, Christians become immobilized, thinking it's enough to simply believe. What are we to do with God's promises? How do we appropriate them, and how does our obedience develop our character? In this session, we will consider the story of Joshua, the Israelite leader who inherited the promise God had given Moses.

1. Have you ever bought or been given something so beautiful or collectible you were afraid to touch it? Share your story briefly with the group.

2. Imagine you got a call today from an attorney who told you a rich uncle had died and left you a fortune. What would you do?

3. Take a few minutes to connect with your spiritual partner or another group member to talk about your spiritual growth. Talk about any challenges you are currently facing in reaching the goals you have set throughout this study. Tell your spiritual partner how he or she has helped you follow through with each step.

GROWING IN YOUR SPIRITUAL JOURNEY   40 MIN.

Maybe he should have known it was coming, but that didn't make it any easier. Moses' death stunned Joshua. What would he do now? For forty years, ever since Moses led them out of Egypt, the Israelites had trekked through the desert, bound for some Promised Land Moses kept telling them about. Now Moses was gone, and they were still in the desert. How could Joshua assure the people that the Promised Land really did exist and wasn't just a figment of Moses' or his imagination?

Then Joshua heard it, as clearly as if Moses himself were sitting on the other side of the tent talking to him. "You and all these people," Joshua heard, "get ready to cross the Jordan River into the land I am about to give them" (Joshua 1:2). Was it God? It must be! It had to be!

Still grieving for his friend and mentor, Joshua rose with renewed faith and confidence. "Be strong and courageous," God had said (verse 6). That meant what Joshua had to do would not be easy. But Joshua had God's promise, "The Lord your God will be with you wherever you go" (verse 9). Because Joshua took God at his word, he found the courage to become the man God intended him to be all along.

Read Joshua 1:1–11:

> *After the death of Moses the servant of the* LORD, *the* LORD *said to Joshua son of Nun, Moses' aide:* ²*"Moses my servant is dead. Now then, you and all these people, get ready to cross the Jordan River into the land I am about to give to them—to the Israelites.* ³*I will give you every place where you set your foot, as I promised Moses.* ⁴*Your territory will extend from the desert to Lebanon, and from the great river, the Euphrates—all the Hittite country—to the Great Sea on the west.* ⁵*No one will be able to stand up against you all the days of your life. As I was with Moses, so I will be with you; I will never leave you nor forsake you.* ⁶*Be strong and courageous, because you will lead these people to inherit the land I swore to their forefathers to give them.* ⁷*Be strong and very courageous. Be careful to obey all the law my servant Moses gave you; do not turn from it to the right or to the left, that you may be successful wherever you go.* ⁸*Do not let this Book of the Law depart from your mouth; meditate on it day and night, so that you may be careful to do everything written in it. Then you will be prosperous and successful.* ⁹*Have I not commanded you? Be strong and courageous. Do not be terrified; do not be discouraged, for the* LORD *your God will be with you wherever you go."* ¹⁰*So Joshua ordered the officers of the people:* ¹¹*"Go through the camp and tell the people, 'Get your supplies ready. Three days from now you will cross the Jordan here to go in and take possession of the land the* LORD *your God is giving you for your own.'"*

4. In verse 2a, one of the first things Joshua needed to face was the reality of Moses' death. How does accepting our circumstances open us to God's perspective for what he has planned for us?

5. Joshua had been Moses' assistant for some time. But with Moses now gone, what role did Joshua suddenly find himself in regarding "all these people"?

6. Have you ever been called into a role that seemed too big for you to do at the time? Briefly share your story and what you believe God taught you through it.

7. How did God reassure Joshua in verse 5? Has God's presence ever sustained you through a difficult time? Share what you learned through the experience with the group.

8. In verse 6, God told Joshua to "be strong and courageous." What special task did God have for Joshua to accomplish?

9. List the specific actions God told Joshua to take in verses 7–8. Why do you think doing those things might require strength and courage?

10. It's easy today to think God's commandments are "just a bunch of rules"—especially in a culture that so often dictates the opposite. What did God promise Joshua as a result of his obedience that helps us see his commands in a different light?

11. After Joshua experienced God's faithfulness in his own life, how was he later able to encourage the soldiers of Israel? (See Joshua 10:16–26, especially verse 25.)

12. How does God use personal experience to give our lives authority before others?

13. Similarly, how does God use personal experience to grow us in godly characteristics, like love or mercy?

14. Share a time when you chose obedience to God's Word over a more popular choice. What happened as a consequence of your decision?

FOR DEEPER STUDY

Joshua's story offers so many rich lessons in leadership, beginning with his response when he found himself in a role he had not specifically sought. He would soon discover that, while Moses had served primarily as a diplomat and shepherd over God's people during their forty-year journey, Joshua's call was to the role of military leader. Yes, God had promised this land to the Israelites, but receiving it would not be a cake walk. Under General Joshua, they had to move in and take what God had given them, conquering one enemy after another.

Examine more lessons from Joshua's leadership style in the verses on page 54:

Joshua 3:5 — What is his example of faith?

Joshua 5:13 – 14 — How did he respond before the man who identified himself as commander of the army of the Lord?

Joshua 8:30 – 32 — How did he follow in Moses' footsteps? (See also Exodus 17:15; 24:4.)

Joshua 11:15 — Describe the legacy of Joshua's life from this verse.

Joshua 24 — Even at the end of his life, how did Joshua continue to serve God before his people?

How do these illustrations from the life of Joshua inspire you?

DEVELOPING YOUR GIFTS TO SERVE OTHERS   10 MIN.

Joshua was specifically gifted to lead the children of Israel into the Promised Land. Have you ever thought of your giftedness as a leadership skill? Whether or not you have the spiritual gift of leadership, as a follower of Christ you lead others in some way. God wants to use whatever you are good at to influence others for his kingdom.

15. Who needs your gifts this week to help them see Jesus? During your prayer time today, ask the group to pray for you as you step out in faith like Joshua did.

16. Take some time now to discuss what's next for your group. Think about whether you will be staying together for another study and what your next study might be. Turn to the Small Group Agreement on pages 89–90 now and talk about any changes you would like to make as you move forward.

SHARING YOUR LIFE MISSION EVERY DAY   10 MIN.

In order to help future generations of Israelites realize God's miraculous victories in delivering them into the Promised Land, Joshua established "stones of remembrance" (Joshua 4:1–9). Sharing these times of God's faithfulness can be a wonderful way to reveal his character and power to others. What has God done in your life or the lives of your loved ones that needs to be memorialized in some way?

17. Consider making some stones of remembrance of your own. How can you use these remembrances to share the power of God with someone who doesn't yet know Christ? Look for an opportunity this week to share with someone what God has done in your life.

SURRENDERING YOUR LIFE FOR GOD'S PLEASURE   15–20 MIN.

18. Where is God asking for obedience from you in a new area? How can the knowledge of his presence help you say yes to his call on your life? Consider Joshua and the children of Israel. Ask the group to pray for you as you choose to be strong and courageous.

19. Allow everyone (who volunteers) to answer this question: How can we pray for you this week? Be sure to write these requests on your Prayer and Praise Report on page 58.

20. Use the Reflections verses at the end of this session in your quiet time this week. Record any thoughts or direction you receive from the Lord in the space provided.

STUDY NOTES

Jordan River. The Jordan River had many different water levels. It still remains as the main waterway from the north to the south of Israel. Some parts of this 200-mile river were easier to cross than others. It has been understood that this section of the river during this time of the year would have been deep and rushing with water. The crossing would have been a test of faith in and of itself and a throwback to the crossing of the Red Sea. Would God provide a path once again? Would it lead anywhere? These questions would clearly have been on the people's minds.

Be strong and courageous. These words in Hebrew, *chazaq* and *amats*, are used almost interchangeably to refer to the inner confidence that comes from believing solely in the promises of God. We often trust God in percentages. The rest is up to us. That kind of trust won't produce the strength and courage to defeat such a foe. This charge is repeated three times. We know that the inhabitants in the land were so intimidating that, without strength and courage, surely the Israelites would not have moved forward to claim what God had given them. The task at hand could easily be perceived as a suicide mission.

Meditate. In Hebrew, the word *hagah* means to imagine, mutter, and roar. Silent reading was almost unknown at that time. Can you imagine if we took this literally today—imagined all that God has done and all that he can do—and then said it, muttered it, roared it all day long? Would it help us to focus on what is true? One South American evangelist has said when it comes to what God can do, our problem is our memory. We tend to forget what he has done for us in the past. Or we can't imagine what else he might do if we called out to him. Meditating on his power could completely change our mind-set in trusting him.

Be prosperous and successful. Prosperity and success are measures of obedience. God does not promise either unless we are willing to do what he says. First Samuel 18:14 reveals that God is the one who grants success. In Nehemiah 1:11, Nehemiah asked God's success in being granted good favor in the presence of the king. We don't find either of these words used to describe material wealth; instead they describe spiritual wealth. God cares more about our spiritual well-being than our financial situation. In Philippians 4:11, Paul reveals a contentment in any situation he finds himself in, yet considers himself always prosperous in the Lord (4:13).

Terrified ... discouraged. Both again are quite interchangeable as they refer to fear related to an object. However, there are hints in the original usage that reveal that "terrified" speaks more to the emotion of fear while "discouraged" speaks more of the outcome of fear. To be terrified is a feeling or attitude of great distress. To be discouraged is to be broken, shattered. They are combined to give force to the concern God has for the people. It would be easy for them to focus on the negative and not on the positive. In Numbers 13:31–33 the people debated the strength and power of the enemy and viewed them as mightier and bigger than themselves. Such an attitude will always lead to defeat. Instead, Joshua and Caleb focused on what God was offering them—a land flowing with milk and honey—and his power to provide (verses 27, 30).

PRAYER AND PRAISE REPORT

Briefly share your prayer requests with the large group, making notations below.
Then gather in small groups of two to four to pray for each other.

Date: _____

PRAYER REQUESTS

_____

_____

_____

_____

_____

_____

_____

_____

_____

_____

_____

_____

PRAISE REPORT

_____

_____

_____

_____

_____

_____

_____

_____

REFLECTIONS

Each day read the daily verse(s) and give prayerful consideration to what you learn about God, his Spirit, and his place in your life. Then record your thoughts, insights, or prayer in the Reflect section. On day six record a summary of what you have learned over the entire week through this study.

DAY 1   *"Be strong and very courageous. Be careful to obey all the law my servant Moses gave you; do not turn from it to the right or to the left, that you may be successful wherever you go. Do not let this Book of the Law depart from your mouth; meditate on it day and night, so that you may be careful to do everything written in it. Then you will be prosperous and successful." (Joshua 1:7–8)*

REFLECT: _____

_____

_____

_____

_____

_____

_____

_____

DAY 2   *"Have I not commanded you? Be strong and courageous. Do not be terrified; do not be discouraged, for the Lord your God will be with you wherever you go." (Joshua 1:9)*

REFLECT: _____

_____

_____

_____

_____

_____

_____

DAY 3   *"As the LORD commanded his servant Moses, so Moses commanded Joshua, and Joshua did it; he left nothing undone of all that the LORD commanded Moses." (Joshua 11:15)*

REFLECT: _____

_____

_____

_____

_____

_____

_____

_____

_____

_____

_____

DAY 4   *"To obey is better than sacrifice, and to heed is better than the fat of rams. For rebellion is like the sin of divination, and arrogance like the evil of idolatry." (1 Samuel 15:22b–23a)*

REFLECT: _____

_____

_____

_____

_____

_____

_____

_____

_____

_____

_____

DAY 5   *"Whoever has my commands and obeys them, he is the one who loves me. He who loves me will be loved by my Father, and I too will love him and show myself to him."* (John 14:21)

REFLECT: _____

_____

_____

_____

_____

_____

_____

_____

_____

_____

_____

_____

DAY 6   Use the following space to write any thoughts God has put in your heart and mind about the things discussed during session four and/or during your Reflections time this week.

SUMMARY: _____

_____

_____

_____

_____

_____

_____

_____

_____

_____

_____

_____

FAITH THAT OVERCOMES — JACOB

Have you ever wanted to shout at God and wondered if it was okay? We all have different impressions of what is appropriate behavior around God, but shouting or shaking one's fist at the sky is probably not on most people's list. Unfortunately this is when piety gets in the way of honesty. If you give it some thought, don't you think that God would prefer honesty, even if it means getting angry? After all, God knows what we think and feel anyway, so to somehow veil our true feelings around him is to be dishonest in the worst way.

This is one of the reasons I like talking to God at the ocean so much. My shouts are drowned out by the ocean roar, and in some ways, that is an answer in and of itself. My arguments around God are pretty much swallowed up by his thundering power.

Think about it this way: God wants a relationship with the real you. If that means wrestling with you all night, well, so be it. I have a feeling he probably likes that. After all, he made us and wants to share in our lives.

Wrestling is a healthy expression between father and son. If I don't wrestle with my kids, something is going to be missing from their character. I can't remember physically wrestling with my father, and I feel a distance around him as a result. That's why I've tried to change that with my own kids. This is one of the ways we learn that conflict is not such a bad thing. One way or another, we're going to have it. The question is: Does it drive us together or drive us apart? Do we grab on even harder to one another, or do we push each other away?

Wrestling is all about gaining physical control over the other person. Now of course we can't do that with God, but in the attempt, we hold on harder, and that's the part he likes. Most good fathers will let their sons win certain concessions at this game anyway, so as not to discourage them or overpower them. I don't think God is any different.

CONNECTING WITH GOD'S FAMILY   20 MIN.

Many of us can relate to the story of Jacob wrestling with God. Through this encounter, Jacob was changed forever. But while

Jacob's wrestling match occurred in one night, God's change in him did not. God's work of transforming Jacob into Israel took a lifetime. In this session, we'll consider, through the life of Jacob, the process of God's character-building work in our lives.

1. What does the word "wrestle" make you think of? Is it always physical? Explain.

2. Take a few minutes to talk about how God has been using this series to develop his character in you. Have you seen him use your gifts in a leadership capacity? What opportunities has God brought your way to invest in the spiritual training of another? Talk about any questions or issues you face with regard to godly character.

3. Sit with your spiritual partner(s), or with another partner if yours is absent. Share how your time in God's Word is going. Discuss any progress you have made on the goals you set in the Grow and Share purposes on the Health Plan. Be sure to record your progress and your partner's progress on page 93.

GROWING TO BE LIKE CHRIST   40 MIN.

After sending his traveling party ahead of him with gifts for his brother Esau, Jacob found himself alone in the camp, alone with his thoughts for the first time in months. Where had he gone wrong? He wasn't a bad guy, was he? After all, his mother, Rebecca, had loved him so much more than his older brother, Esau. Maybe that birthright had rightfully belonged to Esau—but they were twins, after all! It was just a technicality that Esau came out first, right? So how had Jacob ended up in this predicament—running from everyone and deceived for years himself by Laban, his tyrannical father-in-law? Hadn't he worked hard, year after year, to prove his worth?

Now, here he was, finally ready to make things right with his brother and straighten out his life, only to learn that Esau was after him! Could his brother still be angry after all these years? What would happen? How could Jacob's desire to finally do the right thing go so wrong?

Jacob felt a chill in the midnight desert air that cut right to his bones.

"Who are you?" he demanded, stunned by the stranger's sudden appearance. There was something familiar about him. What was it?

Wordlessly, the man approached and locked Jacob in hand-to-hand combat. What was this about? They wrestled for hours — it felt like days to Jacob's weary body. All those years of cattle raising had made Jacob exceptionally strong, but here was a formidable opponent. Still, Jacob wasn't about to quit. Finally, as the sky grew pink with the approaching sunrise, the man, ready to end the conflict, wrenched Jacob's hip out of joint.

"Let me go!" the man exclaimed — and in that moment Jacob realized just who his opponent had been.

"Not until you bless me!" Jacob demanded.

The man leveled a steady gaze at Jacob and quietly asked, "What is your name?"

Broken and ashamed, he confessed the truth. "Jacob," he said. *Heel-catcher; deceiver.*

"No more," said the man. "From this moment on, you are Israel — for you have struggled with God and prevailed."

Limping, Jacob rose and praised God, saying, "I will name this place Peniel — the face of God — because this is where I met God face to face, and he spared my life." God's process of changing Jacob into Israel had begun.

Read Genesis 32:24 – 32:

> *So Jacob was left alone, and a man wrestled with him till daybreak. [25]When the man saw that he could not overpower him, he touched the socket of Jacob's hip so that his hip was wrenched as he wrestled with the man. [26]Then the man said, "Let me go, for it is daybreak." But Jacob replied, "I will not let you go unless you bless me." [27]The man asked him, "What is your name?" "Jacob," he answered. [28]Then the man said, "Your name will no longer be Jacob, but*

Israel, because you have struggled with God and with men and have overcome." ²⁹Jacob said, "Please tell me your name." But he replied, "Why do you ask my name?" Then he blessed him there. ³⁰So Jacob called the place Peniel, saying, "It is because I saw God face to face, and yet my life was spared." ³¹The sun rose above him as he passed Peniel, and he was limping because of his hip. ³²Therefore to this day the Israelites do not eat the tendon attached to the socket of the hip, because the socket of Jacob's hip was touched near the tendon.

4. In Genesis 32:24, we read that Jacob was left alone. What do you think is the significance of this fact to what occurred that night?

5. Can you think of any other examples in Scripture where time spent alone with God impacted his work of change in someone's life? List a few, if possible.

6. Jacob's struggle with God had more to do with admitting who he was and letting God's work of transformation begin than with physical strength. Have you ever wrestled with God in this way? One or two of you briefly share with the group.

7. Persistence is a chief quality evident in all of Jacob's life, not just in this story of his wrestling with God. God encourages persistence. How has your character been developed through some of life's darkest moments?

8. What does Jacob's name change in verse 28 symbolize?

9. In verse 28, the man said to Jacob, "You have struggled with God and with men and have overcome" (some translations say "prevailed"). But was he victorious over God? What do you think the word "prevail" means here? Consider Jacob's own words in verse 30.

10. If you have had a similar experience of wrestling with God and surviving, what new name do you think God has given you?

FOR DEEPER STUDY

It's interesting to note the progression of change in Jacob's life following this landmark event. Once he admitted to God who he was (Genesis 32:27), God's work of change began (32:28). But Jacob still had to settle accounts. Read what happened next in Jacob's life in Genesis 33:1 – 10. What hard work did Jacob still have to do?

Some time later, God revisited Jacob and told him again that his name had been changed to Israel (Genesis 35:9 – 12). Why do you think Jacob needed to be reminded of his new identity?

Jacob's life had been fraught with trouble — much of it his own making. And his new identity did not mean pain was only in his past. He would be a father of nations, yet his own sons would be the cause of his greatest grief as jealous brothers sold Joseph into slavery and convinced their father Joseph was dead. Through it all, Jacob lived to see his son restored to him. Throughout his life, he had many divine encounters with God and his messengers (Genesis 28:10–22; 31:3; 32:1–2, 24–32; 35:1–15; 46:1–4) and clearly served as a model of faith and ultimate triumph. Many scholars believe that at the time of his death, he prophesied the coming of the Messiah (49:10).

How does the story of Jacob, a flawed man who experienced both the lowest and highest spiritual moments one can know, encourage you to persevere in your Christian life?

DEVELOPING YOUR GIFTS TO SERVE OTHERS 10 MIN.

11. What must we do to have a growing, living faith? Like Jacob, we must spend time with God—struggle with him and let him change us. Quiet time alone with the Lord and his Word is one way to do this. Each day we need to set aside time for Bible reading and prayer in order to deepen our knowledge and love for him, which will result in real life change. Turn to How to Have a Quiet Time on pages 99–100 of the appendix for tips about how to spend quality time with the Lord every day.

12. In session two we suggested that you plan to have a party to celebrate Jesus' presence in your group. Have you done that yet? If so, how did it go? If not, set a date now and recruit any help needed to make the party happen.

SHARING YOUR LIFE MISSION EVERY DAY 10 MIN.

13. Do you ever wrestle with God about sharing Christ with someone who needs to know him? Maybe this is someone you don't care for, or someone you think might not like you if you brought it up, or maybe you are just fearful of sharing your faith with anyone. Begin to pray about this and ask God to give you his heart for people and to show you how to begin to obey him. As you obey in this, your faith will grow.

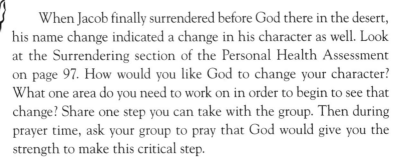

SURRENDERING YOUR LIFE FOR GOD'S PLEASURE   15–20 MIN.

When Jacob finally surrendered before God there in the desert, his name change indicated a change in his character as well. Look at the Surrendering section of the Personal Health Assessment on page 97. How would you like God to change your character? What one area do you need to work on in order to begin to see that change? Share one step you can take with the group. Then during prayer time, ask your group to pray that God would give you the strength to make this critical step.

14. An important way to show love for others is to pray for them. Share your prayer requests in your small group and then take time to pray together. Record your prayer requests on the Prayer and Praise Report on page 71.

15. Use the Reflections verses at the back of this session in your quiet time this week. Record any thoughts or direction you receive from the Lord in the space provided.

STUDY NOTES

Wrestled. Jacob spent his whole life wrestling with God. He had deceived his brother for the birthright and then fled the country out of fear for his own life. He spent many years wondering if he would ever be reconciled to his brother and his God. This was the moment. It took a wrestling match to bring him to a place of brokenness. The location, Peniel (meaning "face of God"), was given by Jacob because this is the place he wrestled with an angelic representation of God (see also Hosea 12:4).

Hip was wrenched . . . limping. Though Jacob won the match, he would never forget this event. God wrenched his hip, causing him to limp the rest of his life. He would never forget the incident and would be marked by this event. Psalm 34:18 says the Lord is near the brokenhearted. God breaks us to bring us to humility (1 Peter 5:6).

Bless me. Jacob wanted desperately a legitimate blessing from the Lord. Eager to serve him in his youthful days, now weathered and seasoned by the trials of life, Jacob was truly ready. We often want a blessing from God early in life. It is not that God withholds it; he waits for the opportune time in our lives to give us direction and insight into our purpose. Jacob's was found in his name. The change of his name was important. It signified the blessing of

God on his life. Jacob would now see himself differently. For an Israelite, a name identified a person with certain identifiable characteristics. Jacob meant *deceiver*. Israel means *he struggles with God* or *God fighter*. Jacob would reenter the land of Canaan with his people stronger and more resolute to fight *for* God, not *with* God.

Briefly share your prayer requests with the large group, making notations below. Then gather in small groups of two to four to pray for each other.

Date: _____

PRAYER REQUESTS

_____

_____

_____

_____

_____

_____

_____

_____

_____

_____

_____

PRAISE REPORT

_____

_____

_____

_____

_____

_____

_____

_____

_____

REFLECTIONS

Each day read the daily verse(s) and give prayerful consideration to what you learn about God, his Spirit, and his place in your life. Then record your thoughts, insights, or prayer in the Reflect section. On day six record a summary of what you have learned over the entire week through this study.

DAY 1   *"Therefore, I urge you, brothers, in view of God's mercy, to offer your bodies as living sacrifices, holy and pleasing to God—this is your spiritual act of worship. Do not conform any longer to the pattern of this world, but be transformed by the renewing of your mind. Then you will be able to test and approve what God's will is—his good, pleasing and perfect will." (Romans 12:1–2)*

REFLECT: _____

_____

_____

_____

_____

_____

_____

DAY 2   *"Therefore we do not lose heart. Though outwardly we are wasting away, yet inwardly we are being renewed day by day. For our light and momentary troubles are achieving for us an eternal glory that far outweighs them all." (2 Corinthians 4:16–17)*

REFLECT: _____

_____

_____

_____

_____

_____

_____

DAY 3   *"Since, then, you have been raised with Christ, set your hearts on things above, where Christ is seated at the right hand of God. Set your minds on things above, not on earthly things. For you died, and your life is now hidden with Christ in God." (Colossians 3:1–3)*

REFLECT: _____

_____

_____

_____

_____

_____

_____

_____

_____

_____

_____

_____

_____

DAY 4   *"Put to death, therefore, whatever belongs to your earthly nature. . . . Because of these, the wrath of God is coming. You used to walk in these ways, in the life you once lived. But now you must rid yourselves of all such things as these." (Colossians 3:5–8a)*

REFLECT: _____

_____

_____

_____

_____

_____

_____

_____

_____

_____

_____

DAY 5   *"Let the peace of Christ rule in your hearts, since as members of one body you were called to peace. And be thankful. Let the word of Christ dwell in you richly as you teach and admonish one another with all wisdom, and as you sing psalms, hymns and spiritual songs with gratitude in your hearts to God. And whatever you do, whether in word or deed, do it all in the name of the Lord Jesus, giving thanks to God the Father through him." (Colossians 3:15 – 17)*

REFLECT: _____

_____

_____

_____

_____

_____

_____

_____

_____

_____

DAY 6   Use the following space to write any thoughts God has put in your heart and mind about the things discussed during session five and/or during your Reflections time this week.

SUMMARY: _____

_____

_____

_____

_____

_____

_____

_____

_____

_____

FAITH THAT ENDURES — JOB

One of Eugene Peterson's many books is called *A Long Obedience in the Same Direction*. Even the title seems long! It's all about endurance. Faith is like the Energizer Bunny; it just keeps on going. Imagine that little bunny, beating on his drum and rolling through every day of your life. That's a silly picture of endurance but you get the idea. And unlike Energizer batteries, this power source never runs out. It just keeps on going ... and going ... and going.

Endurance is one of the most telltale signs of character because it manifests itself over time. There is no shortcut to obtaining it. Endurance is faithfulness proven over time against many obstacles, and those who possess it have earned it. That's a little hard to say about anything spiritual. We don't usually speak about anything as being "earned" in the kingdom of grace, but in the sense that we make choices to continue to believe and stay faithful over time, you could say this character quality is earned. If only because there is no other way to get it.

When I was a student in college, a speaker ended one of his talks in chapel by simply yelling "Keep on!" over and over again. "And when all else fails," he concluded, "keep on!" My roommate and I were so inspired by this that we went back to our room and stenciled "KEEP ON" repeatedly on a roll of adding machine tape that we then stuck all around the walls of our room just under the ceiling. It was a huge motivation for us that year. Keep on believing. Keep on putting yourself in a place where your faith matters. Keep on!

CONNECTING WITH GOD'S FAMILY   20 MIN.

Patience is a noun describing the ability to endure calamity with a spirit of calm. As long ago as 1828, Noah Webster called it "the act or quality of waiting long for justice or expected good without discontent; perseverance; the quality of bearing offenses and injuries without anger or revenge." More than two thousand years ago, God provided a living illustration whose name is Job. However we define it, patience is a quality we all need to make it through even one day of life. In this session, we'll look at Job's patient response to suffering and discover another way in which God grows our character.

1. Describe your typical attitude when you suddenly discover you must wait in a long line.

2. Sit with your spiritual partner(s) and take a few moments to review God's process of change in your life. Where are you—cooperating, resisting, or holding on for dear life? Then be sure to talk about any progress you made in reaching the goals you set during this study.

GROWING TO BE LIKE CHRIST   40 MIN.

If anyone had a "right" to complain, it was Job. Once one of the wealthiest men in all the land of Uz, Job found himself stripped of everything he held dear—his children, his home, his livestock— all his assets wiped out in major disasters. He didn't complain, but patiently accepted the loss.

Over and over, Job's wife said to him, "Why don't you just curse God and die?" (Job 2:9) But Job knew God was good. He didn't understand why he was suffering these incomprehensible losses, but he wouldn't give up on God. Job didn't complain.

Still, he wondered, why *would* God allow this to happen to him? Hadn't he always been faithful? Now here Job was, naked and alone, with nothing left—except God! Job still had God! And God, he realized, was enough.

Job took another look at the God he'd believed in all his life— and in God's light discovered his own spiritual poverty.

Read Job 42:1–6 (Job's confession):

Then Job replied to the LORD: ²"I know that you can do all things; no plan of yours can be thwarted. ³You asked, 'Who is this that obscures my counsel without knowledge?' Surely I spoke of things I did not understand, things too wonderful for me to know. ⁴You said, 'Listen now, and I will speak; I will question you, and you shall answer me.' ⁵My ears had heard of you but now my eyes have seen you. ⁶Therefore I despise myself and repent in dust and ashes."

3. Have someone in the group read Job 40:3 – 5. What was Job beginning to understand at this point?

4. In Job 42:1 – 6, Job admitted to God he had not understood him before. How is our ability to trust God influenced by how well we know him?

5. In Job chapters 4, 5, and 15, we find his "friends" telling him he must have sinned and therefore deserved his fate. As a small group member, what is your responsibility to the others in your group during a time of suffering or hardship?

6. How do you think we can learn to trust God with our unanswered questions?

7. Why do you think it is so hard to see God's plan when we are in the midst of it?

8. How did Job's patient endurance lead to his ultimate understanding of his place before God?

9. Where would an extra helping of patience benefit you right now?

10. What do you think usually happens when we pray for patience?

11. Centuries later, Job's memory was honored by James (James 5:11). Do you think your faithful witness for Christ could make a lasting difference for others? What could you do to make that difference now?

FOR DEEPER STUDY

Read Job 38. What did God want Job—and all of us—to understand about him and about our standing before him?

 DEVELOPING YOUR GIFTS TO SERVE OTHERS   20 MIN.

12. Whether or not you have the patience of Job, we can all develop the ability to endure without complaining. Ask God to show you who in your group or church needs to see patience lived out through you. Plan to do something for that person in a way that might surprise them and let them know God is at work in you.

13. If your group still needs to make decisions about continuing to meet after this session, have that conversation now. Review your Small Group Agreement on pages 89–90 and discuss how well your group study went as well as any changes you want to make as you move forward. Talk about what you will study, who will lead, and where and when you will meet.

SURRENDERING YOUR LIFE FOR GOD'S PLEASURE   15–20 MIN.

14. God was pleased by Job's willingness to endure suffering without complaint. Hopefully, none of us will ever have to endure the level of suffering Job did, but how can you let God know right now that you trust him to lead you in all the ups and downs in your life? Take time in your group to individually express your willing surrender, if you have made such a commitment.

15. Share your prayer requests and record them on the Prayer and Praise Report provided on page 81. Have any previous prayer requests been answered? If so, celebrate these answers to prayer. Then, in simple, one-sentence prayers, submit your requests to God and close by thanking him for his commitment to your relationship and for how he has used this group to teach you more about faith.

16. Use the Reflections verses at the back of this session in your quiet time again this week. Record any thoughts or direction you receive from the Lord in the space provided.

STUDY NOTES

No plan of yours can be thwarted. Job acknowledges God's sovereignty in all things. God most certainly is perceived as being all-powerful but are his plans just as he wishes? Can anything upset his plans? Not according to Job. He learned the single most important lesson about God—everything happens for a purpose according to his plans. Second Samuel 7:28 says, "O Sovereign LORD, you are God! Your words are trustworthy, and you have promised these good things to your servant." God is both sovereign (completely in charge) and trustworthy (he has my best at heart). Even in times of calamity, we can see that God's plans are good because of their result (James 1:2–4).

Obscures my counsel without knowledge. In this phrase, Job reveals a question that God posed to him. Who is the foolish one who questions God's knowledge in ignorance? Job knows the answer. The beginning of our problems is our ignorant question of God's supernatural knowledge. He knows what he is doing and doesn't need to be questioned. It's ignorance that drives us to question God.

Ears had heard of you but now my eyes have seen you. The Bible makes a distinction between hearing and seeing. Many hear the name of God, but have they seen him in action? Do they know him? Seeing is knowing. Job saw with the eyes of his heart. We often feel we know God, but until we can trust him with something big, we'll never know the closeness of his friendship and concern for us (1 Kings 19:12). In Exodus 33:11, it says, "The LORD would speak to Moses face to face, as a man speaks with his friend." Friendship with God is more acute in times of adversity.

Repent in dust and ashes. Job's only response was one of deep contrition for his sinful attitude. Repentance is not simply a change of mind (in Greek, *metanoeo*, literally, "change of mind," Romans 12:2) but also a change of heart (Acts 3:19). This only comes when we see our sin and are willing to acknowledge the consequences. Confession (1 John 1:9) is only as good as the measure of repentance that accompanies it. (See David's confession in Psalm 51:1–4.) Job's repentance led him to a new understanding about God and his purposes.

Briefly share your prayer requests with the large group, making notations below. Then gather in small groups of two to four to pray for each other.

Date: _____

PRAYER REQUESTS

_____

_____

_____

_____

_____

_____

_____

_____

_____

_____

_____

_____

_____

PRAISE REPORT

_____

_____

_____

_____

_____

_____

_____

_____

_____

REFLECTIONS

Each day read the daily verse(s) and give prayerful consideration to what you learn about God, his Spirit, and his place in your life. Then record your thoughts, insights, or prayer in the Reflect section. On day six record a summary of what you have learned over the entire week through this study.

DAY 1   *"Then Job answered the LORD: 'I am unworthy—how can I reply to you? I put my hand over my mouth. I spoke once, but I have no answer—twice, but I will say no more.'" (Job 40:3–5)*

REFLECT: _____

_____

_____

_____

_____

_____

_____

_____

_____

DAY 2   *"Without faith it is impossible to please God, because anyone who comes to him must believe that he exists and that he rewards those who earnestly seek him." (Hebrews 11:6)*

REFLECT: _____

_____

_____

_____

_____

_____

_____

_____

DAY 3 *"But the Counselor, the Holy Spirit, whom the Father will send in my name, will teach you all things and will remind you of everything I have said to you. Peace I leave with you; my peace I give you. I do not give to you as the world gives. Do not let your hearts be troubled and do not be afraid." (John 14:26–27)*

REFLECT: _____

_____

_____

_____

_____

_____

_____

_____

_____

DAY 4 *" 'For my thoughts are not your thoughts, neither are your ways my ways,' declares the LORD. 'As the heavens are higher than the earth, so are my ways higher than your ways and my thoughts than your thoughts. As the rain and the snow come down from heaven, and do not return to it without watering the earth and making it bud and flourish, so that it yields seed for the sower and bread for the eater, so is my word that goes out from my mouth: It will not return to me empty.' " (Isaiah 55:8–11a)*

REFLECT: _____

_____

_____

_____

_____

_____

_____

_____

DAY 5   *"The righteous cry out, and the LORD hears them; he delivers them from all their troubles. The LORD is close to the brokenhearted and saves those who are crushed in spirit." (Psalm 34:17 – 18)*

REFLECT: _____

_____

_____

_____

_____

_____

_____

_____

_____

_____

_____

DAY 6   Use the following space to write any thoughts God has put in your heart and mind about the things discussed during session six and/or during your Reflections time this week.

SUMMARY: _____

_____

_____

_____

_____

_____

_____

_____

_____

_____

_____

APPENDIX

FREQUENTLY ASKED QUESTIONS

WHAT DO WE DO ON THE FIRST NIGHT OF OUR GROUP?

Like all fun things in life—have a party! A "get to know you" coffee, dinner, or dessert is a great way to launch a new study. You may want to review the Small Group Agreement (pages 89–90) and share the names of a few friends you can invite to join you. But most importantly, have fun before your study time begins.

WHERE DO WE FIND NEW MEMBERS FOR OUR GROUP?

This can be troubling, especially for new groups that have only a few people or for existing groups that lose a few people along the way. We encourage you to pray with your group and then brainstorm a list of people from work, church, your neighborhood, your children's school, family, the gym, and so forth. Then have each group member invite several of the people on his or her list. Another good strategy is to ask church leaders to make an announcement or allow a bulletin insert.

No matter how you find members, it's vital that you stay on the lookout for new people to join your group. All groups tend to go through healthy attrition—the result of moves, releasing new leaders, ministry opportunities, and so forth—and if the group gets too small, it could be at risk of shutting down. If you and your group stay open, you'll be amazed at the people God sends your way. The next person just might become a friend for life. You never know!

HOW LONG WILL THIS GROUP MEET?

It's totally up to the group—once you come to the end of this six-week study. Most groups meet weekly for at least their first six weeks, but every other week can work as well. We strongly recommend that the group meet for the first six months on a weekly basis if at all possible. This allows for continuity, and if people miss a meeting they aren't gone for a whole month.

At the end of this study, each group member may decide if he or she wants to continue on for another six-week study. Some groups launch relationships for years to come, and others are stepping-stones into another group experience. Either way, enjoy the journey.

CAN WE DO THIS STUDY ON OUR OWN?

Absolutely! This may sound crazy but one of the best ways to do this study is not with a full house but with a few friends. You may choose to gather with one other couple who would enjoy going to the movies or having a quiet dinner and then walking through this study. Jesus will be with you even if there are only two of you (Matthew 18:20).

WHAT IF THIS GROUP IS NOT WORKING FOR US?

You're not alone! This could be the result of a personality conflict, life stage difference, geographical distance, level of spiritual maturity, or any number of things. Relax. Pray for God's direction, and at the end of this six-week study, decide whether to continue with this group or find another. You don't buy the first car you look at or marry the first person you date, and the same goes with a group. Don't bail out before the six weeks are up — God might have something to teach you. Also, don't run from conflict or prejudge people before you have given them a chance. God is still working in you too!

WHO IS THE LEADER?

Most groups have an official leader. But ideally, the group will mature and members will rotate the leadership of meetings. We have discovered that healthy groups rotate hosts/leaders and homes on a regular basis. This model ensures that all members grow, give their unique contribution, and develop their gifts. This study guide and the Holy Spirit can keep things on track even when you rotate leaders. Christ has promised to be in your midst as you gather. Ultimately, God is your leader each step of the way.

HOW DO WE HANDLE THE CHILD-CARE NEEDS IN OUR GROUP?

Very carefully. Seriously, this can be a sensitive issue. We suggest that you empower the group to openly brainstorm solutions. You may try one option that works for a while and then adjust over time. Our favorite approach is for adults to meet in the living room or dining room, and to share the cost of a babysitter (or two) who can be with the kids in a different part of the house. In this way, parents don't have to be away from their children all evening when their children are too young to be left at home. A second option is to use one home for the kids and a second home (close by or a phone call away) for the adults. A third idea is to rotate the responsibility of providing a lesson or care for the children either in the same home or in another home nearby. This can be an incredible blessing for kids. Finally, the most common idea is to decide that you need to have a night to invest in your spiritual lives individually or as a couple, and to make your own arrangements for child care. No matter what decision the group makes, the best approach is to dialogue openly about both the problem and the solution.

SMALL GROUP AGREEMENT

OUR PURPOSE

To transform our spiritual lives by cultivating our spiritual health in a healthy small group community. In addition, we: _____

_____

_____

_____

OUR VALUES

Group Attendance	To give priority to the group meeting. We will call or email if we will be late or absent. (Completing the Small Group Calendar on page 91 will minimize this issue.)
Safe Environment	To help create a safe place where people can be heard and feel loved. (Please, no quick answers, snap judgments, or simple fixes.)
Respect Differences	To be gentle and gracious to people with different spiritual maturity, personal opinions, temperaments, or imperfections. We are all works in progress.
Confidentiality	To keep anything that is shared strictly confidential and within the group, and to avoid sharing improper information about those outside the group.
Encouragement for Growth	To be not just takers but givers of life. We want to spiritually multiply our life by serving others with our God-given gifts.

Welcome for Newcomers	To keep an open chair and share Jesus' dream of finding a shepherd for every sheep.
Shared Ownership	To remember that every member is a minister and to ensure that each attender will share a small team role or responsibility over time.
Rotating Hosts/Leaders and Homes	To encourage different people to host the group in their homes, and to rotate the responsibility of facilitating each meeting. (See the Small Group Calendar on page 91.)

OUR EXPECTATIONS

- Refreshments/mealtimes _____
- Child care _____
- When we will meet (day of week) _____
- Where we will meet (place) _____
- We will begin at (time) _____ and end at _____
- We will do our best to have some or all of us attend a worship service together. Our primary worship service time will be _____
- Date of this agreement _____
- Date we will review this agreement again _____
- Who (other than the leader) will review this agreement at the end of this study _____

SMALL GROUP CALENDAR

Planning and calendaring can help ensure the greatest participation at every meeting. At the end of each meeting, review this calendar. Be sure to include a regular rotation of host homes and leaders, and don't forget birthdays, socials, church events, holidays, and mission/ministry projects.

Date	Lesson	Host Home	Dessert/Meal	Leader
Monday, January 15	1	Steve/Laura's	Joe	Bill

PERSONAL HEALTH PLAN

This worksheet could become your single most important feature in this study. On it you can record your personal priorities before the Father. It will help you live a healthy spiritual life, balancing all five of God's purposes.

PURPOSE	PLAN
CONNECT	WHO are you connecting with spiritually?
GROW	WHAT is your next step for growth?
DEVELOP	WHERE are you serving?
SHARE	WHEN are you shepherding another in Christ?
SURRENDER	HOW are you surrendering your heart?

DATE	MY PROGRESS	PARTNER'S PROGRESS

SAMPLE PERSONAL HEALTH PLAN

This worksheet could become your single most important feature in this study. On it you can record your personal priorities before the Father. It will help you live a healthy spiritual life, balancing all five of God's purposes.

PURPOSE	PLAN
CONNECT	WHO are you connecting with spiritually? *Bill and I will meet weekly by email or phone*
GROW	WHAT is your next step for growth? *Regular devotions or journaling my prayers 2x/week*
DEVELOP	WHERE are you serving? *Serving in Children's Ministry Go through GIFTS Class*
SHARE	WHEN are you shepherding another in Christ? *Shepherding Bill at lunch or hosting a starter group in the fall*
SURRENDER	HOW are you surrendering your heart? *Help with our teenager New job situation*

DATE	MY PROGRESS	PARTNER'S PROGRESS
3/5	Talked during our group	Figured out our goals together
3/12	Missed our time together	Missed our time together
3/26	Met for coffee and review of my goals	Met for coffee
4/10	Emailed prayer requests	Bill sent me his prayer requests
3/5	Great start on personal journaling	Read Mark 1 – 6 in one sitting!
3/12	Traveled and not doing well this week	Journaled about Christ as Healer
3/26	Back on track	Busy and distracted; asked for prayer
3/1	Need to call Children's Pastor	
3/26	Group did a serving project together	Agreed to lead group worship
3/30	Regularly rotating leadership	Led group worship — great job!
3/5	Called Jim to see if he's open to joining our group	Wanted to invite somebody, but didn't
3/12	Preparing to start a group in fall	
3/30	Group prayed for me	Told friend something he's learning about Christ
3/5	Overwhelmed but encouraged	Scared to lead worship
3/15	Felt heard and more settled	Issue with wife
3/30	Read book on teens	Glad he took on his fear

PERSONAL HEALTH ASSESSMENT

	JUST BEGINNING	GETTING GOING	WELL DEVELOPED

CONNECTING WITH GOD AND OTHERS

I am deepening my understanding of and friendship
with God in community with others. — 1 2 3 4 5

I am growing in my ability both to share and to
show my love to others. — 1 2 3 4 5

I am willing to share my real needs for prayer and
support from others. — 1 2 3 4 5

I am resolving conflict constructively and am
willing to forgive others. — 1 2 3 4 5

CONNECTING TOTAL _____

GROWING IN YOUR SPIRITUAL JOURNEY

I have a growing relationship with God through regular
time in the Bible and in prayer (spiritual habits). — 1 2 3 4 5

I am experiencing more of the characteristics of
Jesus Christ (love, patience, gentleness, courage,
self-control, and so forth) in my life. — 1 2 3 4 5

I am avoiding addictive behaviors (food, television,
busyness, and the like) to meet my needs. — 1 2 3 4 5

I am spending time with a Christian friend (spiritual partner)
who celebrates and challenges my spiritual growth. — 1 2 3 4 5

GROWING TOTAL _____

SERVING WITH YOUR GOD-GIVEN DESIGN

I have discovered and am further developing my
unique God-given design. — 1 2 3 4 5

I am regularly praying for God to show me
opportunities to serve him and others. — 1 2 3 4 5

I am serving in a regular (once a month or more)
ministry in the church or community. — 1 2 3 4 5

I am a team player in my small group by sharing
some group role or responsibility. — 1 2 3 4 5

SERVING TOTAL _____

SHARING GOD'S LOVE IN EVERYDAY LIFE

I am cultivating relationships with non-Christians and praying
    for God to give me natural opportunities to share his love.   1   2   3   4   5

I am praying and learning about where God can use me
    and my group cross-culturally for missions.   1   2   3   4   5

I am investing my time in another person or group who
    needs to know Christ.   1   2   3   4   5

I am regularly inviting unchurched or unconnected
    friends to my church or small group.   1   2   3   4   5

SHARING TOTAL _____

SURRENDERING YOUR LIFE TO GOD

I am experiencing more of the presence and
    power of God in my everyday life.   1   2   3   4   5

I am faithfully attending services and my
    small group to worship God.   1   2   3   4   5

I am seeking to please God by surrendering every
    area of my life (health, decisions, finances,
    relationships, future, and the like) to him.   1   2   3   4   5

I am accepting the things I cannot change and
    becoming increasingly grateful for the life I've been given.   1   2   3   4   5

SURRENDERING TOTAL _____

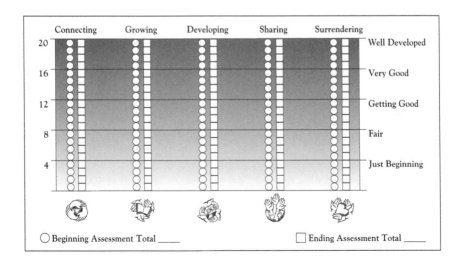

JOURNALING 101

Henri Nouwen says effective and lasting ministry *for* God grows out of a quiet place alone *with* God. This is why journaling is so important.

The greatest adventure of our lives is found in the daily pursuit of knowing, growing in, serving, sharing, and worshiping Christ forever. This is the essence of a purposeful life: to see all five biblical purposes fully formed and balanced in our lives. Only then are we "complete in Christ" (Colossians 1:28 NASB).

David poured his heart out to God by writing psalms. The book of Psalms contains many of his honest conversations with God in written form, including expressions of every imaginable emotion on every aspect of his life. Like David, we encourage you to select a strategy to integrate God's Word and journaling into your devotional time. Use any of the following resources:

- Bible
- One-year Bible
- Devotional book
- Topical Bible study plan

Before or after you read a portion of God's Word, speak to God in honest reflection or response in the form of a written prayer. You may begin this time by simply finishing the sentence "Father ...," "Yesterday, Lord ...," or "Thank you, God, for...." Share with him where you are at the present moment; express your hurts, disappointments, frustrations, blessings, victories, gratefulness. Whatever you do with your journal, make a plan that fits you so you'll have a positive experience. Consider sharing highlights of your progress and experiences with some or all of your group members, especially your spiritual partner(s). You may find they want to join and even encourage you in this journey. Most of all, enjoy the ride and cultivate a more authentic, growing walk with God.

HOW TO HAVE A QUIET TIME

Every relationship takes time to develop. You have to spend time with someone to take a relationship deeper. It's no different with our relationship with the Lord. A quiet time is time alone with Lord. Each day we need to set aside time with him for Bible reading and prayer. As Christians, our primary goal is to become "conformed to the likeness of [Christ]" (Romans 8:29). James writes, "The one who looks steadily at God's perfect law ... and makes that law his *habit*—not listening and then forgetting, but actively putting it into practice will be happy in all that he does" (James 1:25 PH; emphasis added).

FIVE REASONS TO HAVE A QUIET TIME WITH GOD

1. We need nourishment from God's Word to grow.
2. We need to draw close to God.
3. The Word is our best defense against sin.
4. We need to be corrected when we sin.
5. We need encouragement and comfort.

THREE ELEMENTS OF AN EFFECTIVE QUIET TIME

1. Bible reading
2. Prayer time
3. Journaling and Bible note taking

TIPS FOR A MEANINGFUL QUIET TIME

- Recognize that you were created to be in relationship with God and he desires to spend time with you.
- Set a consistent time each day to spend with Jesus. Early morning or evening, children's nap times, and lunch hours are typical times. If your quiet time is scheduled, you are much more likely to keep it.
- Get free from distractions (family members, telephone, TV, email, etc.). Try to eliminate all sounds such as music that might keep you from hearing from God.

- If you miss a quiet time, don't beat yourself up over it. Realize that you got distracted or chose not to have that time that day. Just begin again. The longer you wait, the harder it is to make it a regular habit.
- If your quiet time is dry, difficult, or monotonous, try something new. Consider changing your Bible version, changing your location, listening to the Bible on tape or CD, or changing your routine of reading and praying. Enjoy your time with God.

BEGINNING YOUR QUIET TIME

- Pick a quiet place to meet the Lord that works for you.
- Have your Bible, notebook, and pen with you.
- Start with prayer by asking God to:
  Meet with you
  Prevent distractions
  Reveal his Word for you today
  Bring comfort and clarification for your life
- Read the passage of Scripture you have selected for today.
- Write down some observations from your Bible reading by answering the following two questions:
  What does the passage say generally (what is it teaching me)?
  What does the passage say to me personally (what should I do specifically)?
- Record any insights, thoughts, fears, concerns, praises, or feelings you have from your time with him.
- Respond to God in prayer in the following ways:
  Praise and thanksgiving—"I praise you, God, for ...."
  Repentance and confession—"I confess my sin of ...."
  Ask for guidance—"Lord, lead me today by ...."
  Obedience—"I will obey you in ...."

LEADING FOR THE FIRST TIME

- **Sweaty palms are a healthy sign.** The Bible says God is gracious to the humble. Remember who is in control; the time to worry is when you're not worried. Those who are soft in heart (and sweaty palmed) are those whom God is sure to speak through.
- **Seek support.** Ask your leader, coleader, or close friend to pray for you and prepare with you before the session. Walking through the study will help you anticipate potentially difficult questions and discussion topics.
- **Bring your uniqueness to the study.** Lean into who you are and how God wants you to uniquely lead the study.
- **Prepare. Prepare. Prepare.** Read the Introduction and Leader's Notes for the session you are leading. Consider writing in a journal or fasting for a day to prepare yourself for what God wants to do.
- **Don't wait until the last minute to prepare.**
- **Ask for feedback so you can grow.** Perhaps in an email or on cards handed out at the study, have everyone write down three things you did well and one thing you could improve on. Don't get defensive, but show an openness to learn and grow.
- **Prayerfully consider launching a new group.** This doesn't need to happen overnight, but God's heart is for this to happen over time. Not all Christians are called to be leaders or teachers, but we are all called to be "shepherds" of a few someday.
- **Share with your group what God is doing in your heart.** God is searching for those whose hearts are fully his. Share your trials and victories. We promise that people will relate.

INTRODUCTION

Congratulations! You have responded to the call to help shepherd Jesus' flock. There are few other tasks in the family of God that surpass the contribution you will be making. As you prepare to lead this small group, there are a few thoughts to keep in mind:

Review the "Read Me First" on pages 9–11 so you'll understand the purpose of each section in the study. If this is your first time leading a small group, turn to Leading for the First Time section on page 101 of the appendix for suggestions.

Remember that you are not alone. God knows everything about you, and he knew that you would be leading this group. God promises, "Never will I leave you; never will I forsake you" (Hebrews 13:5b).

Your role as leader. Create a safe warm environment for your group. As a leader, your most important job is to create an atmosphere where people are willing to talk honestly about what the topics discussed in this study have to do with them. Be available before people arrive so you can greet them at the door. People are naturally nervous at a new group, so a hug or handshake can help put them at ease.

Prepare for each meeting ahead of time. Review the Leader's Notes and write down your responses to each study question. Pay special attention to exercises that ask group members to do something other than engage in discussion. These exercises will help your group live what the Bible teaches, not just talk about it. Be sure you understand how an exercise works, and bring any necessary supplies (such a paper or pens) to your meeting.

Pray for your group members by name. Before you begin each session, go around the room in your mind and pray for each member by name. You may want to review the prayer list at least once a week. Ask God to use your time together to touch the heart of every person uniquely. Expect God to lead you to those he wants you to encourage or challenge in a special way.

Discuss expectations. Ask everyone to tell what he or she hopes to get out of this study. You might want to review the Small Group Agreement (see pages 90–91) and talk about each person's expectations and priorities. You could discuss whether you want to do the For Deeper Study for homework before each meeting. Review the Small Group Calendar on page 92 and talk about who else is willing to open their home to host or facilitate a meeting.

Don't try to go it alone. Pray for God to help you, and enlist help from the members of your group. You will find your experience to be richer and more rewarding if you enable group members to help—and you'll be able to help group members discover their individual gifts for serving or even leading the group.

Plan a kick-off meeting. We recommend that you plan a kick-off meeting where you will pray, hand out study guides, spend some time getting to know each other, and discuss each person's expectations for the group. A meeting like this is a great way to start a group or step up people's commitments.

A simple meal, potluck, or even good desserts make a kick-off meeting more fun. After dessert, have everyone respond to an icebreaker question, such as, "How did you hear of our church, and what's one thing you love about it?" Or, "Tell us three things about your life growing up that most people here don't know."

If you aren't able to hold a "get to know you" meeting before you launch into session one, consider starting the first meeting half an hour early to give people time to socialize without shortchanging your time in the study. For example, you can have social time from 7:00 to 7:30, and by 7:40 you'll gather the group with a prayer. Even if only a few people are seated in the living room by 7:40, ask them to join you in praying for those who are coming and for God to be present among you as you meet. Others will notice you praying and will come and sit down. You may want to softly play music from a Life Together Worship CD or other worship CD as people arrive and then turn up the volume when you are ready to begin. This first night will set the tone for the whole six weeks.

You may ask a few people to come early to help set up, pray, and introduce newcomers to others. Even if everyone is new, they don't know that yet and may be shy when they arrive. You might give people roles like setting up name tags or handing out drinks. This could be a great way to spot a coleader.

Subgrouping. If your group has more than seven people, break into discussion groups of two to four people for the Growing and Surrendering sections each week. People will connect more with the study and each other when they have more opportunity to participate. Smaller discussion circles encourage quieter people to talk more and tend to minimize the effects of more vocal or dominant members. Also, people who are unaccustomed to praying aloud will feel more comfortable praying within a smaller group of people. Consider sharing prayer requests in the larger group and then break into smaller groups to pray for each other. People are more willing to pray in small circles if they know that the whole group will hear all the prayer requests.

Memorizing Scripture. Although we have not provided specific verses for the group to memorize, this is something you can encourage the group to do each week. One benefit of memorizing God's Word is noted by the psalmist in Psalm 119:11: "I have hidden your word in my heart that I might not sin against you."

Anyone who has memorized Scripture can confirm the amazing spiritual benefits that result from this practice. Don't miss out on the opportunity to encourage your group to grow in the knowledge of God's Word through Scripture memorization.

Reflections. We've provided opportunity for a personal time with God using the Reflections at the end of each session. Don't press seekers to do this, but just remind the group that every believer should have a plan for personal time with God.

Invite new people. Finally, cast the vision, as Jesus did, to be inclusive not exclusive. Ask everyone to prayerfully think of people who would enjoy or benefit from a group like this. The beginning of a new study is a great time to welcome a few people into your circle. Have each person share a name or two and either make phone calls the coming week or handwrite invitations or postcards that very night. This will make it fun and also make it happen. Don't worry about ending up with too many people — you can always have one discussion circle in the living room and another in the dining room.

SESSION 1: FAITH THAT WORKS — ABRAHAM AND ISAAC

CONNECTING. Questions 1–2. You may not feel you have time to answer both questions 1 and 2. Choose the one that you believe will work best for your group. New groups need to invest time in building relationships with each other. You should be the first to answer the questions while others are thinking about how to respond. Be sure to give everyone a chance to answer the questions, because it's a chance for the group to get to know each other. It's not necessary to go around the circle in order. Just ask for volunteers to respond.

After the icebreaker question, take a moment to pass around a sheet of paper or one of your study guides opened to the Small Group Roster on pages 118–119 so everyone can record their contact information. Have someone make copies to bring to the next group session or someone can type the list and email it to the group this week.

Question 3. A very important item in this first session is the Small Group Agreement. Addressing this will focus the group on the one principle that undergirds this series: A healthy small group balances the purposes of the church: fellowship, discipleship, ministry, evangelism, and worship. Most small groups emphasize Bible study (discipleship), fellowship, and prayer (worship). But God has called us to reach out to others as well. He wants us to *do* what Jesus teaches, not just *learn* about it. You may spend less time in this series studying the Bible than some group members are used to. That's because you'll spend more time *doing* things the Bible says believers should do.

An agreement helps you to clarify your group's priorities and cast new vision for what the group can be. You can find the agreement on pages 89–90. We've found that groups that talk about these values upfront and commit to an agreement benefit significantly. They typically work through conflicts before people get to the point of frustration, so there's a lot less pain.

Take some time to review this agreement before your meeting. Then during your meeting, read the agreement aloud to the entire group. If some people have concerns about a specific item or the agreement as a whole, be sensitive to their questions. Explain that tens of thousands of groups use agreements like this one as a simple tool for building trust and group health over time. Some of the items in the agreement, like "Inviting People" and "Shared Ownership," will become clearer as you move through the sessions. Choose one or two values that you want to emphasize in this study.

Question 4. "Rotating Leaders" is one of the group values we highly recommend for your group. People need opportunities to experiment with ways in which God may have gifted them. Your group will give you all the encouragement you need before, during, and after the session. If you don't plan to continue to lead this group, it is especially important to identify leaders within the group for the next study.

We also suggest you rotate host homes, with the host of each meeting providing the refreshments. Some groups like to let the host lead the meeting each week, while others like to let one person host while another person leads.

You can choose to talk about this here in this session or when we address it again in session three. The Small Group Calendar on page 91 is a tool for planning who will host and lead each meeting. Take a few minutes to plan hosts and leaders for your remaining meetings. Don't pass this up! It will revolutionize your group.

GROWING. If your group is large you may want to start subgrouping to give all members the opportunity to engage in the discussion. Even if someone's answer is difficult to understand, remember that it takes a tremendous step of faith, especially in new groups, to say something early on. Say something like, "Great!" "Thanks!" "That's super!" Then say, "How about somebody else?" "Does anybody else want to share?" Especially if someone starts to dominate the discussion, say, "How about someone who hasn't shared yet?" Keep things bouncing back and forth.

Those who want more Bible study can find plenty of it in this series. For Deeper Study provides more passages you can study on the topic of each session. If your group likes to do deeper Bible study, consider having members answer next week's For Deeper Study section questions ahead of time as homework. Then, during the Growing portion of your meeting, you can share the high points of what you've learned.

Each Growing section begins with an opening story and a passage of Scripture. Have someone read the opening story and someone else read the Bible passage aloud. It's a good idea to ask someone ahead of time, because not everyone is comfortable reading aloud in public. When the passage has been read, ask the questions that accompany it. It is not necessary that everyone answer every question in the Bible study. In fact, a group can become boring if you simply go around the circle and give answers. Your goal is to create a discussion—which means that perhaps only a few people respond to each question and an engaging dialogue gets going.

Question 7. This question opens an opportunity to discuss some ways or experiences that teach us to trust God. You might want to discuss the connection between trust and faith and remind group members that without faith it is impossible to please God (Hebrews 11:6). God was pleased with Abraham because he trusted God's promises and had faith that God would keep them.

Question 10. If you have any question in your own mind that James' claim that faith without works is dead is a contradiction with Paul's insistence that we are justified by faith alone, try to resolve that before the group meets. James is not saying our works are necessary for us to be saved, but he is saying that when we do good things we *prove* we belong to Christ, that we are being led to live as Christ did. In Galatians 2:19–20, Paul too says, "For through the law I died to the law so that I might live for God. I have been crucified with Christ and I no longer live, but Christ lives in me. The life I live in the body, I live by faith in the Son of God, who loved me and gave himself for me." If Christ is living in us, he will work *through* us and he will continue to do the things he did when he walked here.

DEVELOPING. Question 13. Familiarize yourself with the Personal Health Assessment before the meeting. You may want to take the assessment yourself ahead of time and think about your goal. Then you can give group members a real-life example of what you are actually committed to doing. We also encourage you to complete a simple goal under each purpose. Ask your coleader or a trusted friend to review it with you. Then you'll understand the power of this tool and the support you can gain from a spiritual partner.

Offer this assessment in a spirit of grace. It should make people hungry to see the Holy Spirit work in their lives, not ashamed that they're falling short. Nobody can do these things in the power of the flesh! And sometimes the most mature believers have the clearest perception of the areas in which they need considerable help from the Spirit.

Question 14. For many, spiritual partners will be a new idea. We highly encourage you to pair up with someone for the six weeks of this study. It's so hard to start a spiritual practice like prayer or consistent Bible reading with no support. A friend makes a huge difference. Partners can check in with each other weekly either at the beginning of your group meetings or outside the meeting. As leader, you may want to prayerfully decide who would be a good match with whom. We call this connection a "spiritual partnership." Remind people that this partnership isn't forever; it's just for a few weeks.

Take time to get familiar with the Personal Health Plan on pages 92–93 so you can offer help with it if group members need explanation. This is a great tool for tracking your goals for growth with your spiritual partner.

SHARING. Question 15. The Circles of Life represent one of the values of the group agreement: "Welcome for Newcomers." Some groups fear that newcomers will interrupt the intimacy that members have built over time. However, groups generally gain strength with the infusion of new blood. It's like a river of living water flowing into a stagnant pond. Some groups remain permanently open, while others open periodically, such as at the beginning and ending of a study. Love grows by giving itself away. If your circle becomes too large for easy face-to-face conversations, you can simply form a second discussion circle in another room in your home.

As leader, you should do this exercise yourself in advance and be ready to share the names of the people you're going to invite or connect with. Your modeling is the number-one example that people will follow. Give everyone a few moments in which to write down names before each person shares. You might pray for a few of these names on the spot and/or later in the session. Encourage people not to be afraid to ask someone. Almost no one is annoyed to be invited to something! Most people are honored to be asked, even if they can't make it. You may want to hand out invitations and fill them out in the group.

We encourage an outward focus for your group because groups that become too inwardly focused tend to become unhealthy over time. People naturally gravitate to feeding themselves through Bible study, prayer, and social time, so it's usually up to the leader to push them to consider how this inward nourishment can overflow into outward concern for others. Never forget: Jesus came to seek and save the lost and to find a shepherd for every sheep.

Encourage everyone to write at least one name in one of the circles. Be sure to take time to pray for the group and for those whose names have been written down.

SURRENDERING. Questions 16–17. Encourage the group to begin to pray together if that isn't happening yet. Never pressure a person to pray aloud. That's a sure way to scare someone away from your group. Instead of praying in a circle (which makes it obvious when someone stays silent), allow open time when anyone can pray who wishes to do so. Have someone write down everyone's prayer requests on the Prayer and Praise Report (page 21). If your time is short, consider having people share requests and pray just with their spiritual partners or in smaller circles of three or four.

Question 18. Remind the group about the importance of spending time alone with God throughout the week. Mention that the Reflections section can be an opportunity for developing this important habit while using this study.

SESSION 2: FAITH THAT LISTENS — MARY AND MARTHA

In order to maximize your time together and honor the diversity of personality types, do your best to begin and end your group on time. You may even want to adjust your starting or stopping time. Don't hesitate to open in prayer even before everyone is seated. This isn't disrespectful of those who are still gathering — it respects those who are ready to begin, and the others won't be offended.

Have everyone sit back, relax, close their eyes, and listen to one of the songs on a LIFE TOGETHER Worship CD, or any worship CD. You may want to sing the second time through as a group, or simply take a few moments of silence to focus on God and transition from the distractions of your day.

CONNECTING. Questions 1–2. You will get to know each other more quickly if you spend time with an icebreaker question at each session. Choose one of these questions that you think best suits your group. This is a great opportunity for bonding within your group.

Question 3. Checking in with your spiritual partners will be an option in all sessions from now on. You'll need to watch the clock and keep these conversations to five to ten minutes depending on how much time is available. Encourage everyone to use the Personal Health Plan on pages 92–93 to help them stay accountable for their spiritual growth. If partners want more time together (as is ideal), they can connect before, after, or outside meetings. Give them a two-minute notice and hold to it if you ever want to get them back in the circle! If some group members are absent or newcomers have joined you, you may need to help people connect with new or temporary partners. In a week or two, you might want to ask the group how their partnerships are going. This will encourage those who are struggling to connect or accomplish their goals.

GROWING. Have someone read the opening story and someone else read the Bible passage aloud. It's a good idea to ask someone ahead of time, because not everyone is comfortable reading aloud in public. When the passage has been read, ask the questions that accompany it.

Review the questions and choose ones you believe will be most helpful for your group. As you work through this section, try to help the group see the importance of balance. We don't want those who have the gifts of helping to feel that it is not a good gift. And we don't want those who have the worship gifts to think that they don't ever have to help others. Balance is key. Try to help the group to see what a life of balance between the two can look like in everyday life. Remember it is not necessary that everyone answer every question in the Bible study.

DEVELOPING. As leader, you're in the people development business. Part of your job is to help others discover and develop their gifts. You may not need their help to host or lead a meeting, but they need you to let them take on a role and support them so that they succeed. If you have children, you know that it's often easier to do a job yourself than to help someone else learn to do it. But that's what Jesus did with his disciples, and it's what he wants us to do for those we lead. If you have identified someone in your group who has the gift of hospitality or organization, ask them to plan and host the party mentioned in question 11.

SHARING. Question 12. Before your group meets, take time to fill in the "WHEN are you shepherding another in Christ?" on your Personal Health Assessment on page 92. Be prepared to share your next step with the group to initiate discussion.

SURRENDERING. There are bound to be people in your group who long for healing, whether physical or emotional, so be sure to save time to pray for each other. Follow your church's practice in the way you approach this exercise. If you're concerned that some members might confuse or try to "fix" others through prayer, pray as a whole group and monitor how people pray. But don't be overly concerned: the very worst that will happen is that someone will pray in a way that distresses someone else. If that happens you can simply talk to each person privately before your next meeting. As leader, you set the example of how people will pray for each other in your group, and most members will follow your lead.

Remind the group to use their Prayer and Praise Report on page 32 to keep track of prayer requests and answers to prayer. Also mention that finding balance between doing and worship is important. Whether or not they use the Reflections and Scripture we have provided in this study, spending time each day in God's Word and in prayer is a good response to this study.

Remember to maximize your time together and honor your group by doing your best to begin and end your group on time. Announce opening prayer, even before everyone is seated, to signal the group that you are ready to begin.

If you've had trouble getting through all the Bible study questions, consider breaking into smaller circles of four or five people for the Bible study (Growing) portion of your meeting. Everyone will get more "airtime," and the people who tend to dominate the discussion will be balanced out. A circle of four doesn't need an experienced leader, and it's a great way to identify and train a coleader.

CONNECTING. Questions 1–2. We have provided two questions that can serve as icebreakers. Choose the one that works best for your group. Remember that your group may become boring if you require every group member to answer every question. Two or three responses are plenty. Also remember that if people are silent before they answer, it's because they're thinking!

GROWING. Don't forget to ask a couple of people to read the opening story and the Bible passage for you. Since some people are not comfortable reading aloud in public, ask ahead of time.

Be sure to review the questions beforehand and choose the ones that will be most meaningful for your group.

DEVELOPING. Question 11. Developing your group members' gifts and abilities is important. Be on the lookout for ways to encourage everyone to take an active role in running and leading the group. If you haven't yet addressed rotating leaders and host homes, turn to the Leader's Notes for session one on page 106 for help about this important leadership development practice for your group.

SHARING. Question 13. In the Sharing section of session one we asked everyone to write some names on the Circles of Life diagram on page 19. Make sure you take time to encourage the group to give a report of how things went. If they haven't followed through yet, ask them to commit to a specific time, maybe even within the next twenty-four hours.

SURRENDERING. Question 16. Be sure you manage the group's time so there is opportunity to share prayer requests and pray together. This is one of the most important habits necessary to bond your group.

Question 17. Continue to remind the group of the importance of spending daily time with the Lord. The Reflections section is a very good way to do this.

SESSION 4:
FAITH THAT OBEYS — JOSHUA

CONNECTING. Choose either question 1 or 2 to open your group.

GROWING. As you prepare to lead this lesson, look for ways you can help the group recognize the importance of obedience to God and how it relates to faith. Obedience says God is trustworthy and that we believe he is a worthy recipient of our loyalty. Both our trust and obedience prove our faith in him. Without faith it is impossible to please God (Hebrews 11:6).

DEVELOPING. Question 16. In this session we want you to begin thinking about the future of this group. Begin to talk about whether your group will continue to meet and what you might study next. If you have time, consider reviewing your Small Group Agreement on pages 89 – 90 to see if you met your group goals and if you want to make any changes as you move forward.

SHARING. Question 17. Look ahead at this question and consider making this into an exercise for the group. Maybe you can get some smooth stones and have some permanent markers available for the meeting. Have the members write what they want to remember on their stone. The stones can serve as a reminder of something important God has done for them. Challenge the group to share with each other how God has worked in their lives.

SURRENDERING. Question 18. Give the group time to pray for the courage to respond to anything new to which God might be calling them. Also pray for any prayer requests.

SESSION 5:
FAITH THAT OVERCOMES — JACOB

CONNECTING. Overcoming faith can be a difficult concept to grasp, depending on one's past experiences and/or level of Christian maturity. Prepare the group for this discussion by reminding them that overcoming difficult times and experiences bring big rewards in spiritual growth.

Questions 1–2. Choose the icebreaker question you prefer and allow group members to connect with their spiritual partner(s).

GROWING. Question 4. Jacob was a man with a large family and many servants and cattle. It's likely he was almost never alone, a fact that makes this incident even more singular. If any of your group members are new to Scripture, you might want to make sure they're aware of who Jacob is. Mention his past as well: he'd been a deceiver who had stolen his brother's birthright, but had then spent many years in the service of a deceitful man. Laban, father of his beloved Rachel, had promised Jacob this daughter and then given him her older sister, Leah, on his wedding night. Jacob had to work an additional seven years to earn Rachel! He was a man who had learned his lessons the hard way—and one more was about to come upon him.

Question 5. If your group gets stalled on this question, help them by offering an example or two. One is found in the story of Elijah's escape from Jezebel in 1 Kings 19:1–18. Note God's mercy on this terrified prophet during an especially low spiritual moment. See how Elijah discovered the presence of God during this time of isolation. Another example is David, who used his times alone—either watching his sheep or running from Saul—to draw close to God by writing psalms. Get the group to suggest things that help us feel close to God during times of solitude.

Question 6. Wrestling with God, of course, does not necessarily refer to a physical contest like the one Jacob experienced. Our wrestling can be in the times before we accepted Christ, struggling to believe; it can appear in times of doubt even after salvation, or during especially difficult trials. Encourage the group to explore this idea and bring out its depth.

Question 7. Plan to briefly share an example of your own to begin this discussion of God in the dark moments of life—be ready for some emotion on this question from some of your members. Remember people are more important than a lesson. Give time to those who need the support of the group.

Question 8. Use this question as a springboard to talk about the importance of having our identity firmly rooted in Christ.

Question 9. Whenever you see a question that uses the words "what do you think," as this one does, encourage group members to realize this is not a true/false or multiple choice question. All ideas are valid.

Question 10. This question is intended for reflection and can be skipped unless someone is eager to share their new name!

DEVELOPING. Question 11. In order to help people grow in their relationship with God, we have provided an exercise to help those who desire to deepen their quiet time with him. Before the session familiarize yourself with the How to Have a Quiet Time section on pages 99–100 so you can explain it to the group as you look at it together.

SESSION 6:
FAITH THAT ENDURES — JOB

You made it! Since this is the last session in this study, ask if the members would like to plan a party to celebrate. Sharing times of achievement is a good way to measure growth, and what better way to rejoice than with a group get-together!

GROWING. Question 3. Take a few minutes to examine the few verses before the passage addressed in this question. This will help you to better understand the context. If your Bible has footnotes or other references, taking a few moments to look those up will also help you guide the group discussion.

Question 4. Help the group to understand that knowledge of God is critical if we are to have the ability to trust him. We can gain knowledge about him through Scripture, but only through experience can we truly know God. Our ability to trust God grows through times of testing, as he proves himself worthy over and over again.

Question 5. On the surface, this looks like an easy answer — but when it comes to application, it's not easy at all. Talk about barriers that often keep us from being genuine friends.

Question 8. We usually can't see what God has in mind until we have endured and survived. Often, it is years down the road before we realize what God was doing.

Questions 9 – 10. Be warned! When we ask for patience, it is usually put to the test — which is how patience is developed.

SURRENDERING. Question 16. In this final session, the verses chosen for the Reflections section are especially rich. Encourage group members to spend time meditating on these verses and journaling them, thinking back on not only this session, but all the lessons in this study. Where can you be more like Christ in your character? Let these verses guide your growth.

SMALL GROUP ROSTER

Name	Address	Phone	Email Address	Team or Role	Church Ministry
Bill Jones	7 Alvalar Street L.F. 92665	766-2255	bjones@aol.com	Socials	children's ministry

(Pass your book around your group at your first meeting to get everyone's name and contact information.)

Name	Address	Phone	Email Address	Team or Role	Church Ministry

Experiencing Christ Together:

Living with Purpose in Community

Brett & Dee Eastman; Todd & Denise Wendorff; Karen Lee-Thorp

Experiencing Christ Together: Living with Purpose in Community is a series of six, six-week study guides that offers small groups a chance to explore Jesus' teaching on the five biblical purposes of the church. By closely examining Christ's life and teaching in the Gospels, the series helps group members walk in the steps of Christ's early followers. Jesus lived every moment following God's purposes for his life, and Experiencing Christ Together helps groups learn how they can do this too. The first book lays the foundation: who Christ is and what he has done for us. Each of the other five books in the series looks at how Jesus trained his followers to live one of the five biblical purposes (fellowship, discipleship, service, evangelism, and worship).

	Softcovers	DVD
Beginning in Christ Together	ISBN: 0-310-24986-4	ISBN: 0-310-26187-2
Connecting in Christ Together	ISBN: 0-310-24981-3	ISBN: 0-310-26189-9
Growing in Christ Together	ISBN: 0-310-24985-6	ISBN: 0-310-26192-9
Serving Like Christ Together	ISBN: 0-310-24984-8	ISBN: 0-310-26194-5
Sharing Christ Together	ISBN: 0-310-24983-X	ISBN: 0-310-26196-1
Surrendering to Christ Together	ISBN: 0-310-24982-1	ISBN: 0-310-26198-8

Pick up a copy today at your favorite bookstore!

Doing Life Together series

Brett & Dee Eastman; Todd & Denise Wendorff;
Karen Lee-Thorp

Based on the five biblical purposes that form the bedrock of Saddleback Church, Doing Life Together will help your group discover what God created you for and how you can turn this dream into an everyday reality. Experience the transformation firsthand as you begin Connecting, Growing, Developing, Sharing, and Surrendering your life together for him.

"Doing Life Together is a groundbreaking study . . . [It's] the first small group curriculum built completely on the purpose-driven paradigm . . . The greatest reason I'm excited about [it] is that I've seen the dramatic changes it produces in the lives of those who study it."

—From the foreword by Rick Warren

Small Group Ministry Consultation

Building a healthy, vibrant, and growing small group ministry is challenging. That's why Brett Eastman and a team of certified coaches are offering small group ministry consultation. Join pastors and church leaders from around the country to discover new ways to launch and lead a healthy Purpose-Driven small group ministry in your church. To find out more information please call 1-800-467-1977.

	Softcover	
Beginning Life Together	ISBN: 0-310-24672-5	ISBN: 0-310-25004-8
Connecting with God's Family	ISBN: 0-310-24673-3	ISBN: 0-310-25005-6
Growing to Be Like Christ	ISBN: 0-310-24674-1	ISBN: 0-310-25006-4
Developing Your SHAPE to Serve Others	ISBN: 0-310-24675-X	ISBN: 0-310-25007-2
Sharing Your Life Mission Every Day	ISBN: 0-310-24676-8	ISBN: 0-310-25008-0
Surrendering Your Life for God's Pleasure	ISBN: 0-310-24677-6	ISBN: 0-310-25009-9
Curriculum Kit	ISBN: 0-310-25002-1	

Life Together Student Edition

Brett Eastman & Doug Fields

The Life Together series is the beginning of a relational journey, from being a member of a group to being a vital part of an unbelievable spiritual community. These books will help you think, talk, dig deep, care, heal, share ... and have the time of your life! Life ... together!

The Life Together Student Edition DVD Curriculum combines DVD teaching from well-known youth Bible teachers, as well as leadership training, with the Life Together Student Edition Small Group Series to give a new way to do small group study and ministry with basic training on how to live healthy and balanced lives-purpose driven lives.

STARTING to Go Where God Wants You to Be-Student Edition — ISBN: 0-310-25333-0
CONNECTING Your Heart to Others'-Student Edition — ISBN: 0-310-25334-9
GROWING to Be Like Jesus-Student Edition — ISBN: 0-310-25335-7
SERVING Others in Love-Student Edition — ISBN: 0-310-25336-5
SHARING Your Story and God's Story-Student Edition — ISBN: 0-310-25337-3
SURRENDERING Your Life to Honor God-Student Edition — ISBN: 0-310-25338-1

Small Group Leader's Guide Volume 1 — ISBN: 0-310-25339-x
Small Group Leader's Guide Volume 2 — ISBN: 0-310-25340-3
Small Group Leader's Guide Volume 3

Pick up a copy today at your favorite bookstore!

We want to hear from you. Please send your comments about this book to us in care of zreview@zondervan.com. Thank you.

ZONDERVAN.com/
AUTHORTRACKER
follow your favorite authors